Richard Ingrams was born in 1937. His father was the head of Black Propaganda in the Second World War; his maternal grandfather was Queen Victoria's doctor. Educated at Shrewsbury and Oxford, Ingrams was one of the founders of *Private Eye* in 1961, becoming editor the following year, a post which he held for over twenty years. In 1992 he helped to launch *The Oldie* magazine which he edited until 2014. He has written regular weekly columns for the *Observer* and later the *Independent* and was a panellist on the BBC's *News Quiz* for many years. His books include biographies of William Cobbett and Malcolm Muggeridge, a memoir of John Stewart Collis and a number of anthologies including *England*, *The Best of Beachcomber* and *Jesus: Authors Take Sides*.

LUDO AND THE POWER OF THE BOOK

Ludovic Kennedy's Campaigns for Justice

Richard Ingrams

Constable • London

CONSTABLE

First published in Great Britain in 2017 by Constable
This paperback edition published in 2018

1 3 5 7 9 10 8 6 4 2

A CIP catalogue record for this book
is available from the British Library.

ISBN: 978-1-47210-908-8

Typeset in Sabon by SX Composing DTP, Rayleigh, Essex
Printed and bound in Great Britain by Clays Ltd, St Ives plc

Papers used by Constable are from well-managed forests
and other responsible sources.

Constable
An imprint of
Little, Brown Book Group
Carmelite House
50 Victoria Embankment
London EC4Y 0DZ

An Hachette UK Company
www.hachette.co.uk

www.littlebrown.co.uk

For Sara.
With love and thanks for all her help.

Contents

Foreword

'Ludo' . . . there you have it in one word. The abbreviated and affectionate name says it all and, without more, conveys the measure of the man: authoritative yet accessible. Passionate and perceptive. Courageous and encouraging. Unique and unforgettable.

This book is a fine testament to a breed long gone, to a tradition of investigative journalism for which there appears to be no longer time, nor space, nor resources. The world wide web and social media have all played a deadly role in submerging analysis and elevating the soundbite. The information superhighway is now so fast-moving that it's difficult to distinguish matters of substance from flights of fancy or even latterly fake news.

The techniques of challenging inquiry, diligence, persistence and careful research employed by Ludo are set out here in intimate detail. They demonstrate how he achieved effective results and his unassailable reputation.

While there have since been pockets of remarkable work akin to Ludo's, overall there is a pressing need to resurrect his approach. It is no coincidence that the award for investigative and campaigning journalism established by the *Guardian* and *Private Eye* in memory of another journalistic titan, Paul Foot, was discontinued in 2014 after ten years. Whatever the rationale for its termination, the celebration of courage, tenacity and reasoned argument is vital. David Conn's remorseless pursuit of truth and justice for the Hillsborough victims and now Orgreave survivors in his regular *Guardian* columns exemplifies the point.

It was Ludo's initial foray into the then barely developed legal hinterland of miscarriages of justice that captured my attention and imagination. In 1961, *Ten Rillington Place* was published. It had an enormous formative impact on my thinking while I was still at university which has endured until now.

This seminal book challenged the rectitude of a murder conviction. A young man with considerable learning difficulties, called Timothy Evans, was wrongfully hanged. The real culprit was a special constable and serial killer, John Christie. The rigour of the intellectual battle that Ludo had to fight and the odds he had to face were formidable. It was instrumental in the debate which led to the abolition of capital punishment and a pardon for Evans. As I read this compelling narrative I realised what was possible if you were passionate and committed. It provided hope and inspiration for those moments of despair and desperation – situations only too familiar to those of us constantly in struggle on the judicial front line. So for me it set the example and the standard. In the words of Mahatma Gandhi, 'Be the change you wish to see in the world'. In large part it's why I became a barrister.

It was not just for me but for numerous others that Ludo unlocked doors to mental and physical freedom. Literally for the Birmingham Six whose appeals he followed assiduously. He attended the court hearings regularly and it was during these pressured years that I got to know him and benefit from his supportive words of advice. Whilst at the time I was regarded as some sort of 'red under the bed', the same could certainly not be said of him.

He had blazed a trail that had demonstrated that verdicts in the criminal system were not written on tablets of stone. There was a whole string of appeals besides the Six which took place during the 80s and early 90s which forced a reappraisal of the system. Two different Cardiff Three appeals; the Tottenham Three; Judith Ward; M25; Guildford Four. As a result, the Criminal Cases Review Commission was established in 1995, beginning work in 1997.

This process was assisted by a burgeoning high profile television documentary series: *World in Action*, *Rough Justice* and *Trial and Error*. Despite the irritation of their lordships in the Court of Appeal (Lane and Taylor) it must be remembered that there has never been adequate resources to fund the necessary research and preparation for the important initial stages of either an application for leave to the Court of Appeal or to Commission. The role of these programmes was absolutely vital in the same way as Ludo's writings were. Ludo himself was an experienced TV presenter and recognised their significance. Like the demise of the investigative journalist, however, these televisual investigations have also faded save for sporadic one-offs and specials (recently, *Lawful Killing* – Duggan; and *Smears* – Hillsborough).

The lessons of the criminal arena have subsequently spread far wider and by the time of Ludo's death in 2009 his message of resilience and inquisition was permeating many other areas of injustice, and has continued to do so. Victims and survivors of disparate and harrowing circumstances have begun to take issue with the official version of events – Lawrence (murder); the Marchioness disaster (Thames collision); Bloody Sunday (killing by British troops); Chilcot (legality of military service in Iraq); Leveson (unlawful media intrusion and hacking); and Hillsborough (ninety-six deaths at a football match).

The forces at work are powerful: the need to know; establishing the truth in a transparent and public manner; and above all enforcing accountability, a feature sadly lacking in our democratically bankrupt society. Without exception, the principal objective is to ensure, so far as is humanly possible, the prevention and avoidance of repetition. In other words, it is done for the benefit of those that come after.

These are all values which Ludo espoused and promoted through his work. His influence cannot be underestimated and his mark will remain indelible for all those who care about access to justice in a time of searing austerity.

Michael Mansfield QC, December 2016

Of all the duties of the historian, the most sacred is, that of recording the conduct of those who have stood forward to defend helpless innocence against the attacks of powerful guilt.

William Cobbett

Introduction

I first met Ludovic Kennedy (universally known as 'Ludo') in 1963, the year of the Profumo scandal and the assassination of President Kennedy; the year I took over the editorship of *Private Eye*. I was introduced to him by Malcolm Muggeridge, a colleague of his on the BBC's *Panorama* programme. At the time both were members of a breakaway group of BBC journalists hoping to set up an independent film-making organisation called TRI (Television Reporters International) with the aim of making programmes and selling them to the BBC or ITV. It was an idea ahead of its time and in the end nothing came of it.

Despite their age difference, Malcolm and Ludo were two of a kind. Both of them mavericks and troublemakers, they shared a low opinion of television, particularly the BBC, for which they worked on and off for most of their lives. They would have preferred to be known primarily as writers – between them they wrote thirty or forty books – but because of the widespread but ephemeral fame that TV bestows they were known as television personalities, and when they ceased to appear on TV they were undeservedly forgotten.

I remember going to meet with Ludo and Malcolm in a pub in Old Compton Street, just around the corner from the *Private Eye* office at 22 Greek Street. Ludo, handsome, charming and without any sign of self-importance, had been covering the trial of Stephen Ward, a central figure in the Profumo scandal, at the Old Bailey, and was planning to write a book about it. In his view Ward, an osteopath patronised by smart upper-class patients, had been the victim of a shameful miscarriage of justice, as a result of which he had committed suicide, dying in hospital after he was found guilty, *in absentia*, of living off immoral earnings. Ludo's book *The Trial of Stephen Ward* was eventually published the following year, 1964.

The Stephen Ward story was the real scandal of the Profumo affair. Profumo himself resigned after admitting to lying to the House of Commons in denying that he had had an affair with 'good-time girl' Christine Keeler. He might have survived had not the Home Secretary Henry Brooke instigated a police investigation into Profumo's friend Ward, who, until then, had backed up his denial. (I knew something personally about this as Ward had at one point come round to *Private Eye*'s office, on Profumo's behalf, to find out what, if anything, we knew about the story – the answer was not very much – and to assure us that Profumo had been telling the truth to the House when he denied any affair with Keeler.) Ward's subsequent trial was brilliantly described by Ludo, who sat through the whole proceedings, fuming over the pomposities of the lawyers and their hypocritical puritanism when confronted by the sexual libertine Ward. (Prosecuting counsel Mervyn Griffith-Jones was already famous for asking the jury in the *Lady Chatterley* trial whether it was a book they would wish their wife or servants to read.) Ludo's indignation increased when the legal authorities in the person of the Lord Chief Justice, Lord Parker, refused to provide him with a transcript of the trial – a sign that there was official unease about the prosecution.

For me, then aged twenty-five, the story had been an eye-opener, revealing the corruption that lay behind the bland façade of British politics and confirming my doubts about the integrity of the police and the law courts, which Ludo had already exposed in his book *Ten Rillington Place*, published in 1961 – the year *Private Eye* was first published.

My generation, which launched *Private Eye* and the satirical TV programme *That Was the Week That Was*, is often credited with the demolition of the old Establishment and the traditional deference accorded to the likes of politicians, judges and policemen. But I would argue that Ludo played a much more influential role in that process. He and TV colleagues like

Robin Day were the first to interview politicians man to man; but, more importantly, in *Ten Rillington Place* he exposed the failings of the legal system, the police force and the politicians who oversaw them. And unlike the Angry Young Men then lashing out savagely in all directions, he did so quietly, while making every allowance for the pressures under which the authorities operated. But the inescapable truth at the end of it – that an innocent man had been hanged – was dynamite compared with the satirical barbs of us teenage marksmen and played a major part in the eventual abolition of capital punishment in Britain.

Sometime after that first meeting Ludo interviewed me on television. After all these years I can't recall what was said. But I remember Ludo as the best interviewer I ever came across (with the possible exception of Mavis Nicholson). He did it partly by being, or appearing to be, completely relaxed and therefore making me feel the same way. Many years later I had the same experience when I appeared once or twice on his most successful programme *Did You See?* He gave the impression, one critic remarked, that he had just popped into the BBC 'on his way to the club'. (He used *On My Way to the Club* as the title of his memoirs, published in 1989.)

Throughout the seventies and eighties I found myself increasingly involved in legal matters (mostly libel actions), experiencing all the frustrations familiar to anyone who gets engaged willingly or unwillingly in litigation. It created a bond with Ludo, who in his books and articles exposed better than anyone the fallible nature of British justice, castigating the incompetence and arrogance of the judges. Some of the judges who feature in this book were the same men that I myself came across in my almost always disastrous law court battles. For example, Sir Daniel Brabin, the judge who presided over the second government inquiry into the Rillington Place murders, was also the judge in a bizarre libel action brought by two *Sunday People* reporters against *Private Eye* in 1969. In both cases Brabin managed to reach the wrong verdict when the truth was staring him in the face.

As a result of his writing, Ludo became the inspiration for a small band of journalists who devoted themselves to exposing miscarriages of justice, including Chris Mullin, Bob Woffinden, David Jessel (mainstay of the BBC's *Rough Justice* programme) and my close friend and *Private Eye* colleague Paul Foot. Working with Paul – most notably while he was investigating and writing about the A6 murder, for which James Hanratty was wrongly executed in 1962, and the murder of newspaper boy Carl Bridgewater in 1978 – taught me two things about these miscarriage-of-justice stories. One was the length of time, often many years, it took to rectify the errors of the courts and secure the release of the wrongly convicted.

The other was that when all the details of these stories came to light piecemeal, a book was needed at the end of the day to bring everything together. But even that was not enough. The book had to be read to have any effect. Ludo and Paul were successful not only because of their detective skills but because they were masterful writers. In particular, they were able to go through the transcript of a trial, much of which is devoted to irrelevant issues and legal red herrings, and seize on the vital elements, thereby creating a narrative that made sense and carried the reader along.

Both Paul and Ludo had their critics. As a Marxist, Paul was accused of having a political agenda aimed at discrediting the courts and the police force. Likewise, Ludo was more than once charged with seeking to avenge his father, a naval officer who had himself been the victim of a miscarriage of justice (this charge was scarcely justified as Ludo only uncovered the story that led to his father's dismissal late in life).

What is much more relevant is that in all the cases in which they were involved, including the four recounted here, Ludo, like Paul, was instinctively indignant about the wrongful imprisonment – or execution, in two of the cases – of the innocent, and felt an irresistible urge to help them and those campaigning for justice, usually their wives and mothers. It made no difference that the victims might be criminals, as were Paddy Meehan in the Ayr case and Cooper and McMahon in the Luton

Post Office case. If all heaven were put in a rage, as William Blake said over the imprisonment of a robin in a cage, Ludo felt the same kind of rage about a man spending long years in prison for a crime he didn't commit.

It would be wrong to claim that Ludo acted alone as a knight in shining armour when he undertook to investigate a miscarriage of justice. He was helped in every case by the convicted man's lawyers, their relatives and particularly by sympathetic journalists. A number of these have helped me in compiling this tribute, in particular Gareth Peirce, Bryan Magee, Patrick Marnham, Bob Woffinden, Martin Short, John Shirley, Magnus Linklater, Tom Mangold, Sue Crowther, Will Wyatt, Joe Beltrami, Wendy Mantle, Len Murray and David Scott.

I am grateful to Charlotte Fairbairn, who provided me with her father's voluminous scrapbooks and the typescript of an interesting, but anonymous book about the Meehan case; Roly Keating and Eddie Mirzoeff, who helped procure a number of recordings of BBC TV programmes; and Edda Tasiemka, whose cuttings library provided invaluable assistance.

Chapter 1

Timothy Evans

The first the world heard of Ludovic Kennedy was when he married Moira Shearer in February 1950. A huge crowd had collected at Hampton Court, where the reception was held, with a bevy of press photographers and gossip writers. Their attention was focused exclusively on Moira, a beautiful redheaded ballet dancer internationally famous as the star of the Powell and Pressburger film *The Red Shoes*. Little was written about the bridegroom, who was described in one press report as 'a young writer and lecturer at Ashridge College'[1] (an adult education institute in Hertfordshire). Photographs showed a handsome young man smiling benignly at the camera. Eton and Oxford, served in the Navy in the war – nobody seemed to know much about him, though fellow males might have been envious of his landing such a prize catch as Moira Shearer.

---

[1] Source unknown.

Had they probed a little deeper, the gossip columnists could have uncovered a story rather at odds with the perceived picture of Ludovic Kennedy as a good-looking, privileged deb's delight. Life had not been as easy for him as his charming, well-groomed appearance might have suggested. Born into the Scottish upper class, he had grown up with an unaffectionate mother who had used every opportunity to criticise and do him down. His father, a naval officer whom he hero-worshipped, had been drummed out of the service after a court-martial found him guilty of failing to deal with a mutiny in the ranks. Recalled in 1939, he was made captain of a ship, the *Rawalpindi*, which was sunk by German torpedoes in the first naval action of the war.

Ludo himself was already in the Navy when his father died. After seeing action against the *Bismarck*, he served as aide-de-camp to the Governor of Newfoundland, where he began to experience severe depression for the first time. His symptoms would continue for the next twenty-five years despite regular visits to expensive psychiatrists, many of whom attributed his illness to his mother's hostility – but such was his carefree manner that few friends or colleagues were aware of what he was going through.

Writing in 2002, Ludo referred to his 'lifelong obsession with miscarriages of justice'.[2] But it wasn't

---

[2] *Thirty-six Murders and Two Immoral Earnings.*

really like that. The 31-year-old who married Moira Shearer was uncertain about where his life was leading. His book in diary form, *One Man's Meat*, which chronicles his life in the early 1950s, including his engagement and marriage, contains all kinds of observations about personal, literary and political matters, but nothing at all about crime and punishment or miscarriages of justice. If he had an obsession of any kind at this time it was more to do with writing – what it was like to be a writer, the writers he admired (Somerset Maugham in particular) – while the blurb could boast that Ludovic Kennedy (pictured in a literary pose with cigarette and bow tie) 'is already well known as the author of two books, *Sub-lieutenant* and *Nelson's Band of Brothers*'.

He was thirty-six when he began to investigate miscarriages of justice, and then it was more as a result of a succession of chance events than any kind of driving 'obsession'. And, once he had discovered from experience just what was involved in fighting for an innocent victim and having, like others, to earn a living and support a family, he more than once vowed that he would have no more to do with it, only to be drawn back in as the result of a chance meeting or, in the case of Anna Hauptmann, a chance sighting of her on a hotel-room TV set in America.[3]

---

[3] See Chapter 4, below.

In these cases Ludo almost always found himself fighting a lone battle, supported only by loyal relatives and concerned lawyers. But in the case that indirectly led to his series of crusades – the Craig/Bentley case – he was one of thousands crying out for justice. This case became one of the most controversial in legal history and played an important role in the eventual abolition of capital punishment.

One night in November 1952, two youths, Christopher Craig and Derek Bentley, attempted a raid on a confectionery warehouse in Croydon, and during a rooftop stand-off with a posse of policemen Craig shot and killed one of the officers, PC Sidney Miles. Craig, though younger than Bentley, was the dominant partner, but because he was sixteen he escaped the death penalty. The 19-year-old Bentley was not so fortunate, even though the police had already apprehended him by the time PC Miles was shot. In view of the obvious anomaly, it was widely assumed that Bentley would be reprieved, and when his appeal failed there were nationwide protests. Nevertheless, there remained the possibility of a reprieve being granted by the Home Secretary, Sir David Maxwell Fyfe,[4] and Ludo and Moira sent a telegram to Maxwell Fyfe, pleading for clemency, discovering afterwards that thousands of

[4] Maxwell Fyfe later became Lord Kilmuir after Harold Macmillan sacked him in the 1962 reshuffle known as the 'Night of the Long Knives'.

others had done the same. But he refused to give way and Bentley was hanged. Later, Ludo took revenge of a sort by describing Maxwell Fyfe as 'a Scot whose arrogance matched his ignorance' and repeating a couplet that he claimed was going round the Inns of Court at the time: 'The nearest thing to death in life is David Patrick Maxwell Fyfe'. [5]

The Craig/Bentley case was a good example of the way such stories refuse to die, particularly if there are determined people prepared to carry on the struggle for reparation – in this case Bentley's sister Iris, who campaigned ceaselessly for a posthumous pardon. Lord Bingham eventually granted that pardon in 1998 (too late for Iris Bentley, who had died the previous year) and also made a ferocious attack on his predecessor Lord Goddard, the 'hanging and flogging' judge who had sentenced Craig and Bentley. As with Maxwell Fyfe, Ludo took obvious pleasure in this, adding some insults of his own when writing about the case. He described meeting Goddard at a dinner party given by the right-wing historian Arthur Bryant. Hoping to gain some insights into the law, he was disappointed when Goddard spent the whole evening telling dirty jokes. For good measure, when looking back on the case, Ludo suggested that Goddard was in the habit of masturbating when pronouncing the death sentence

---

[5] 'On My Way to the Club' (McFyfe poem).

(the same charge was made by George Orwell in *Like It Was: The Diaries of Malcolm Muggeridge*).

Iris Bentley pursued her campaign to the accompaniment of a regular flow of books, TV programmes, newspaper articles and even songs about the case. As late as 1992, forty years after the murder, yet another book was published. Written by M. J. Trow with a foreword by Ludo, it was titled *Let Him Have It, Chris*. Over the intervening four decades these five words – which Bentley allegedly shouted before Craig fired the fatal shot – had become famous in legal history because they led directly to Bentley's conviction and execution, despite the obvious fact that they were ambiguous.

As with so many of these stories, Mr Trow's book was the result of a chance meeting. In the summer of 1988 his wife was taking driving lessons with an instructor whose name was Ray Pain. Learning that his pupil was the wife of a writer, Mr Pain revealed that his 80-year-old father Claude had been one of the policemen on the warehouse roof the night PC Miles was shot. Feeling the need to unburden himself after long years of silence, Claude Pain told Trow that his presence on the roof had never been disclosed in court. He had made a deposition of his evidence at the time but remained one of three policemen present at the crime scene who were never called as witnesses and, soon after, the deposition and his notebook 'disappeared'. The reason was obvious: unlike the three officers – Harrison, Fairfax and McDonald

– who had claimed to have heard Bentley shout, 'Let him have it, Chris', Pain had stated categorically in his deposition that he never heard him say anything of the sort, even though he was standing next to Bentley at the time. Had Pain given evidence at the trial, it is possible that Bentley would have been acquitted, especially if his story had been taken in conjunction with what Craig's counsel, John Parris, subsequently wrote in his memoirs.[6] There Parris pointed out that in a very similar case (R *v.* Appleby, 1940), in which two men were held jointly responsible for the shooting of a police officer by one of them, Appleby incited his partner with almost identical words to those allegedly used by Bentley: 'Let him have it, he is all alone.' That was either an extraordinary coincidence or proof that the evidence against Bentley was, at the least, deeply suspect.

Writing in 2002, Ludo had no doubt that the policemen had lied in the witness box and that Craig had never uttered the words 'Let him have it, Chris'. But part of his strength as a reporter in such cases was his custom always to try to understand the motives of officers caught up, in this case, in a situation where one of their own had met his death at the hands of a violent criminal:

One does not have to imagine that when the three officers sat down together to prepare their depositions and discuss

[6] John Parris, *Most of My Murders*.

the evidence they would give, they consciously and deliberately agreed to put into Bentley's mouth words they knew he had never said. It does not happen like that. More likely, in my view, one of the officers remembered the words said to have been uttered in the Appleby case. Probably therefore one of the three officers on the roof, without mentioning the Appleby case, had said something like 'Am I imagining this or did I hear Bentley shout just before Craig fired "Let him have it"?' And the other two, perhaps grateful for the lead and such being the power of self-delusion, would have agreed that yes, now they cast their minds back, they were sure that Bentley had said something of the sort. Let us not forget that the death of their much-loved and respected colleague Sidney Miles had traumatised them (the shot that had hit him could equally well have hit one of them). Deep in the unconscious they wanted a life for a life and if it could not be extracted from the defendant who had killed Miles, then his partner in crime would do just as well.[7]

In such an atmosphere it would have taken a braver man than Claude Pain to have broken ranks. As he admitted in a revealing disclosure to M. J. Trow, 'Some very funny things were going on in those days, Mr Trow. I could be hit by a car or anything.'[8]

---

[7] *Thirty-six Murders and Two Immoral Earnings.*

[8] M. J. Trow, *Let Him Have It, Chris.*

Ludo's conjectures about the evidence against Bentley will be dismissed by his critics as mere speculation, but we should remember that they were written at the end of a career in which he had acquired unique insights into the workings of policemen. Fifty years earlier, when the trial of Craig and Bentley took place, and before his eyes had been opened to police malpractice, his feelings were different. In 1952, Ludo had no misgivings about the evidence presented in court. He even wrote that Bentley took no part in the shooting 'apart from shouting encouragements to Craig'.[9] In other words, the young Ludo, who had no obsession with miscarriages of justice, was quite happy about the policemen's evidence. It was only the death sentence that aroused his indignation.

Ludo admitted that three or four years previously he might not have felt the same indignation. But as a result of being commissioned to write a series of articles on prison conditions for the *Sunday Times*, he had been forced to confront the reality of capital punishment. Then came the Craig/Bentley trial and Ludo, still unsure of his role as a writer, wrote a play called *Murder Story,* whose central character, Jim Tanner, was loosely based on Bentley. It was surprisingly successful at the time, with a provincial tour and a brief West End run, but revisited today it presents Tanner in an

---

[9] *One Man's Meat*, 1953.

absurdly sentimental light as a gentle and illiterate half-wit. Small wonder that Bentley's father, who attended the first night, was disapproving. Witness this exchange between Tanner and the prison chaplain in the con-demned man's cell:

Jim:	What's God like? What's he look like?
Chaplain:	Different people see him in different ways. Nobody knows because nobody's ever seen him. Many people think of him as a very old man, a very kindly old man with a long white beard, rather like Father Christmas.
Jim:	Father Christmas! I like that. Do you see him like that?
Chaplain:	Yes, Jim, I think I do.
Jim:	And he's waiting for me?
Chaplain:	Yes, he's waiting for you.

When Victor Gollancz published the play in 1956, Ludo added a long appendix on the subject of capital punishment that showed him to be a much better pamphleteer than playwright. Some of the arguments were familiar – the failure of capital punishment to act as a deterrent, for example. What was unusual was the emphasis Ludo placed on the effects suffered by those who had to carry out the executions. In his play he had done his best to convey this aspect – 'one which is rarely considered and discussed'. But the real-life testimonies he quotes in the appendix have a much greater impact:

a prison doctor reveals, 'I have never seen anyone who had anything to do with the death penalty who was not the worse for it,' while a former prison governor speaks of their sense of shame, 'I felt quite unclean after having taken part in a hanging.'[10] It was plain that Ludo shared the same feelings of revulsion towards a barbaric ritual as those whose responsibility it was to carry it out. Supporters of hanging might have been reassured by the evidence of the hangman Albert Pierrepoint, who told a committee of inquiry that after hanging hundreds of victims he 'no longer turned a hair'. But Ludo drew exactly the opposite moral: 'Here, then, is a man, the licensee of a public house in the Midlands, who on behalf of us all has during the last twenty years killed *some hundreds* of men and women, and has become so inured to it that he does not "turn a hair". Have we the right to allow any man to degrade himself so?'[11]

Along with hundreds of other plays, *Murder Story* is now forgotten. But it was responsible for the chance sequence of events that put Ludo on the road to self-fulfilment. One of those who saw the play was an old friend of Ludo's from Oxford, George Scott, who since leaving university had become editor of the political magazine *Truth*. In 1954 the magazine published a profile entitled 'Literary Man about Town', in which

---

[10] *Murder Story.*

[11] *Murder Story.*

Scott poked gentle fun at his friend, calling him 'a young fogy [*sic*]' and referring to 'the embarrassingly inaccurate reproduction of working-class life in his moving and sincere play'. But it was thanks to Scott having seen and written about the play that, when a few months later a book called *The Man on Your Conscience* by Michael Eddowes landed on Scott's desk, he immediately thought of Ludo as a possible reviewer. The subject matter echoed the Craig/Bentley story, Eddowes, a retired solicitor, claiming that a young Welshman called Timothy Evans had been hanged in 1950 for a murder committed by another man, John Christie.

The book, Ludo quickly decided, was appallingly written. This perhaps was not surprising, given that it was the work of a lawyer. Eddowes, who mysteriously referred to himself throughout as 'we', began by saying he was dealing with a mystery, only to state two pages later that there wasn't really a mystery after all. But if there wasn't any longer a mystery there was now a problem, and 'in view of the complexity of the problem and in order to understand the text it is as well that the reader should read all the appendices'.[12] There were *thirteen* of these, comprising well over half of the book. Ludo, one of the few to persist, read Eddowes's book three times before he fully grasped what the poor man was trying to say. It was worth the effort, for what he

---

[12] Michael Eddowes, *The Man on Your Conscience*.

was trying to say was that in 1950 the authorities had hanged an innocent man. It was a tragic and terrible story, but Mr Eddowes was not qualified to tell it.

Ludo reviewed the book, at the same time resolving to investigate the story himself when he was ready for it. He had always wanted to write, even as a boy, though he had been discouraged by his nautical father, who told him that writing was something he could do perfectly well in his spare time. At Oxford after the war he had been greatly influenced by his tutor, the Professor of English (Lord) David Cecil, whose enthusiasm for literature was infectious. At the same time he joined the university's Writers' Club, which invited authors to address its regular meetings. One of them was Evelyn Waugh who, when asked by Ludo how he could hope to earn a living while writing a book or play, replied, unhelpfully, 'Be a road sweeper.'

At the time he received Michael Eddowes's book for review, Ludo was already a published author. There was his play *Murder Story*, a memoir of his early life in the Navy, *Sub-lieutenant* (1942), and his diary, *One Man's Meat* (1953). But a proposed sequel to *Sub-lieutenant* had failed to find a publisher and the reviews of *One Man's Meat* had been lukewarm, one critic, Maurice Richardson, comparing it to 'the memoirs of a septuagenarian postmaster'.[13] And in the meantime there

---

[13] *Observer*, date unknown.

were urges pulling Ludo in other directions. In 1955, when Eddowes's book was published, independent television was launched amid a great deal of opposition, providing, for the first time, competition to the BBC. Ludo was recruited by one of the new commercial companies, ATV, to compère a magazine programme with the unimaginative title *Sunday Afternoon*. It was not a very exciting prospect but it gave him an entry into television – something, he said later, that he had 'long been seeking'. There was probably nothing more behind this than an instinctive feeling that he would be good at it, and this proved to be the case. Ludo looked good on the screen and, being completely relaxed himself, was able to make those he interviewed feel relaxed as well – a rare and enviable gift. He now offered his services to Independent Television News (ITN), which was developing a more informal approach to news broadcasting than that of the hidebound BBC. Here he was working alongside Robin Day, the egotistical, bow-tied broadcaster who pioneered a new and aggressive technique of political interviewing that later became the norm.

Day's attitude symbolised the general loss of respect for the Tory Establishment that burgeoned after Anthony Eden's disastrous Suez adventure in 1956, when he attempted – with the help of the French and the Israelis – to regain control of the Suez Canal after it was nationalised by the Egyptian President Gamal Abdel Nasser. The protests, similar in some ways to those that greeted Tony Blair's invasion of Iraq in 2003, propelled many young men into politics for the first time, including Ludo himself. 'What triggered me off,' he said later, 'was the horror of Suez – the terrible unbelievable thing that we were sending gunboats out to the canal – "to have a go at the Wogs". I thought I must protest about this.'[14] In his role as an ITN newscaster he refused to follow the Foreign Office instruction to refer to the landing of British troops in Egypt as an 'intervention' rather than an invasion, and was supported in this by his boss, Sir Geoffrey Cox.

Dissatisfied, for various reasons, with the two main political parties, both Robin Day and Ludo joined the Liberal Party. Jo Grimond, who took over the leadership of the party in 1956, was bound to appeal to Ludo as the two men had so much in common, both being young, good-looking, charming, Old Etonian and Scottish. From Grimond's point of view, Ludo was ideal parliamentary candidate material, having a well-known face (thanks to TV), not to mention a famously beautiful film star as a wife. 'Ludovic Kennedy,' Grimond explained in an overenthusiastic vein, 'has been driven by generous passion to plunge into politics in protest against the needless and dangerous divisions in national life.'[15] Ludo himself seemed equally carried away, announcing in the

---

[14] *Radio Times*, 2 December 1979.

[15] *On My Way to the Club*, p. 245.

Sunday Dispatch: 'There sometimes comes a time in a person's life when he feels himself being pushed by some inner force in a certain direction . . . however upsetting the move, however uncertain the consequences. That moment has just arrived in my life.'[16]

But it proved to be a false dawn. Selected to stand as the Liberal candidate in a by-election in Rochdale, Ludo beat the Tories into third place but the seat was won by Labour and the same thing happened in the General Election the following year when Labour won again, albeit with a reduced majority. Ludo could take comfort only in the fact that Robin Day, who stood at Hereford, had been equally unsuccessful.

Events were forcing Ludo back to what he knew he most wanted to do and what he most enjoyed doing – 'the choosing of some voluntary project on which to work alone – studying and making notes on it, then writing about it'.[17] In his book *One Man's Meat* he had quoted Flaubert with approval: 'One is not free to write this or that. One does not choose one's subject.' His friend George Scott had advised him 'to keep within the limits of the world he knows'.[18] Yet, paradoxically, it was Scott who had sent him Michael Eddowes's book, a book about murder, execution and corruption set

---

[16] *On My Way to the Club*, p. 245.

[17] *On My Way to the Club*, p. 245.

[18] 'Truth' profile.

in a squalid London slum. And ever since reading and reviewing that book he had been haunted by the face of Timothy Evans – 'hunted, hopeless' – and felt the need finally to untangle the story from all the irrelevancies and red herrings. He might not have been aware of it but in all the cases he took on, always by chance, he had the knack of seeing, almost at once, what the story was. In this case it was that Timothy Evans – hanged for murder in 1950 – was, and had to be innocent. It should have been obvious to everyone, but it wasn't.

Ludo called his book, when he eventually finished it, *Ten Rillington Place* – an inspired idea because the house itself was central to the story. Long since demolished, with even the name Rillington Place wiped from the map, it had been a ramshackle, run-down slum of a house – more than once Ludo described it as a dolls' house – in an obscure corner of Notting Hill long before that area became a fashionable nesting place for Hooray Henrys and Sloane Rangers. Though divided into separate two-room flats on three floors, it was so small, according to Ludo's account, that if there had been grass instead of concrete in the front you could have jumped from the top flat without suffering any injury. It had a narrow wooden staircase and an outside toilet shared by three tenants (there was no bathroom in the house). The first-floor flat was vacant; Evans, his wife Beryl and baby Geraldine occupied the top flat; and Mr and Mrs Christie the ground-floor flat. At the time the Evanses came to Rillington Place, no living person apart from Christie was aware that the tiny 'garden' at the rear of the house contained the bodies of two women murdered by Christie in the early 1940s.

Christie, the compulsive strangler and necrophile who moved into Rillington Place in 1938, was one of seven children of a skilled carpet designer and founder member of the Halifax Conservative Party and his wife née Halliday (Ludo doesn't give her Christian name). It was 'a solid Victorian middle-class family'. Bullied by his sisters and his disciplinarian father and spoiled by his mother, he became a shy, introspective boy who was afraid of women and kept himself to himself. In 1916, aged eighteen, he was called up for army service in the First World War. Two years later, six months before the Armistice, he was ordered to France, where he was hit by a mustard-gas shell, which he later claimed had left him blinded and unable to speak for several months. At the trial of Timothy Evans Christie was to use this story very effectively to gain sympathy from the court, but Ludo, with typical thoroughness, made a study of the effects of mustard gas and found nothing in Christie's records to suggest that he had ever been blinded. He further concluded that the loss of voice was due not to mustard gas but to shellshock.

Later it surprised those whose perception of Christie was of a respectable middle-class citizen to learn that he had a substantial criminal record. In 1921 he had been sentenced to nine months' imprisonment for stealing postal orders when working for the Post Office, and two years later he was prosecuted again for obtaining money under false pretences. In September 1924, he received a six-month prison sentence for larceny. He was disowned by his family and temporarily separated from his wife Ethel, whom he had married in 1920.

Striving to explain Christie's complex make-up, Ludo fell back on the familiar stereotype of Jekyll and Hyde – the classic dual personality created by his fellow Scottish storyteller Robert Louis Stevenson. Christie/Jekyll, in this instance, was a polite, well-spoken married man who took off his hat to ladies in the street. Christie/Hyde 'came out at night, the frequenter of squalid cafés, the consort of pimps and prostitutes'.[19] It was not surprising that 'Hyde' had had six criminal convictions in all. What was extraordinary was that his record had not prevented 'Jekyll' from being recruited as a special constable in the War Reserve Police in 1939. He served in that role for four years, during which time he committed his first murder. His victim was a 17-year-old student nurse from Austria, Ruth Fuerst, who had taken to part-time prostitution. Living in a bedsitter only a few minutes' walk from Rillington Place, she may have met Special Constable Christie when he was

---

[19] *Ten Rillington Place.*

patrolling his beat. They struck up a relationship of sorts and Christie strangled her while they were having intercourse, then buried her body in the tiny garden at the back of the house. Ethel was visiting her family in Sheffield at the time. The following year, he killed his second victim, Muriel Eady, in the same way.

Christie, as Ludo probably rightly surmised, would have been excited by the arrival at 10 Rillington Place (four years after the death of Muriel Eady) of Evans with his pretty 18-year-old wife Beryl, three months pregnant at the time. Evans, then aged twenty-three, had been born in Merthyr Vale, South Wales, in 1924. As a result of a boyhood foot injury while bathing in the River Taff, he had spent many years in and out of hospitals and never learned to read or write. His father left home shortly before he was born and was never heard of again. His mother, to whom Ludo dedicated his book, remarried a Mr Probert. After the family moved to London in 1935 Evans, his mother and his sisters remained in regular contact, all living in the Notting Hill area. Despite being credited with a low IQ, Evans – who was slight in build and only five feet two inches tall (Ludo calls him 'a tiny little fellow') – was quite shrewd and managed to hold down a number of jobs. One employer described him as 'quick, reliable, punctual and honest'. But he was no match for John Christie, no match for Inspectors Black and Jennings or Mr Christmas Humphreys QC.

The Evanses' daughter was born in October 1948 – six months after they had moved into Rillington Place – and was christened Geraldine, but only a few months later Beryl found she was pregnant once again. The prospect of coping with two small children in their tiny flat filled both parents with alarm, and despite opposition from her husband Beryl made no secret of the fact that she was seeking an abortion (then an illegal operation). Thus it was that news reached the ears of Christie, who saw it as a wonderful opportunity to gratify his insane urges. He therefore posed to both parents as a man with considerable medical knowledge and experience who knew how to perform an abortion. Evans was strongly against the idea and the couple quarrelled – relations between them had been strained for some time. But Beryl was adamant and instructed Christie to go ahead with the operation, thereby sealing her fate. With Evans out at work, Christie laid Beryl on the floor and gassed and strangled her, while attempting, but, he said, not succeeding in having, intercourse with her. When Evans returned from work later in the day Christie told him that unfortunately the abortion had not gone according to plan and that Beryl had died. Together, they moved the body into the vacant flat on the first floor. Christie, who had total control over Evans, warned him not to involve the police as they would both be prosecuted. He also advised him to leave London, saying he would place baby Geraldine in the care of a couple he knew in East Acton and dispose of Beryl's body in the main drain. Evans believed him on every count and left to stay with his aunt and uncle in Merthyr Tydfil, leaving Christie free to strangle baby Geraldine, who was bound to lead to questions about the whereabouts of her mother – the couple in East Acton were an invention – and dump the body along with that of Beryl in the disused washhouse at the rear of the house.

Finding it more and more difficult to cope with a life of deception and worried about his baby daughter, Evans eventually went to the police in Merthyr Tydfil, telling them that his wife had died from taking pills to bring about an abortion and that he had put the body down a drain. The Notting Hill police were alerted and could find no body whereupon Evans made a second statement in which he gave a truthful account of what had happened, as far as he understood it. When the Notting Hill police searched 10 Rillington Place for the second time they discovered the two bodies in the washhouse. Interrogated by the police, Christie made the most of his former service in the force to win them over and expressed incredulity at Evans's description of him as an amateur abortionist, adding that Evans had been on very bad terms with Beryl, who had confided to Mrs Christie that he had even threatened to kill her.

Evans was brought back to London in police custody.

A press photographer – who must have been tipped off by the police – snapped him as he arrived at Paddington Station. The resulting picture, showing a startled Evans dwarfed on either side by two burly policemen – Inspectors Jennings and Black – later preyed on Ludo's mind and eventually convinced him to write his book. Evans was taken to Notting Hill Gate police station, where he was informed that the bodies of his wife and baby had been discovered, that they had both been strangled, and that he was being held responsible for their deaths.

In a state of shock and grief and after hours of intense interrogation Evans subsequently made a long and detailed confession to Chief Inspector Jennings and Detective Inspector Black which was to prove fatal to him. He was later charged but, for legal reasons, only with the death of Geraldine, though the judge allowed evidence about Beryl's death to be introduced.

In *Ten Rillington Place* Ludo devoted three whole chapters to an account of Evans's trial, which opened on 11 January 1950 and lasted for three days. As in all the cases recounted in this book, he made a meticulous examination of the transcript of the trial, noting all the evasions and omissions, the giveaway signs of bias, not to mention the lies. Generally sympathetic to police and jurymen and well aware that the barristers made the best of the brief they were given, he reserved his sharpest criticism for judges, generally clever and well-educated men whose duty it was to be impartial. In this respect Mr Justice Lewis, who presided over Evans's trial, lamentably failed, though Ludo was kind enough to point out more than once that he was a sick man who lived for only a few days after the trial. The judge's most crucial failing was the extent to which he was beguiled by the prosecution's chief witness, John Reginald Halliday Christie. Christie, who stoutly denied all of Evans's accusations, dismissed the abortion story as a fantasy, and successfully passed himself off (with the help of prosecuting counsel Mr Christmas Humphreys, a tall, slim Buddhist who held that Shakespeare's plays were written by the Earl of Oxford) as a veteran of the First World War who had been gassed and blinded and who ever since had suffered from ill health, so that even giving evidence at the Old Bailey was a physical ordeal for him (full of sympathy, Mr Justice Lewis allowed him to sit down in the witness box).

Was it remotely possible that this man – 'this old contemptible. This war-wounded hero, this pillar of the police force, this paragon of respectability'[20] (as Ludo mockingly described him) – was it possible that such a man with so many physical handicaps could strangle a healthy young woman, help Evans to carry her corpse to the flat below, and later single-handedly haul her body

---

[20] *Ten Rillington Place.*

to the washhouse in the backyard? It was not surprising that the jury took only forty-five minutes to reach their verdict of guilty. An appeal was subsequently dismissed by three judges, Mr Justice Sellers, our old friend Lord Goddard (see page 19) and Mr Justice Humphreys, father of the prosecuting counsel at the Old Bailey. Evans later described the judges, with justification, as 'bloody old sods'.

Evans's confession was the biggest obstacle facing Ludo when it came to convincing his readers – exactly the same obstacle that had faced Evans's lawyers when it came to convincing the jury of his innocence. Why would an innocent man confess to a crime that would almost certainly result in his execution by hanging? Nowadays, when so many false confessions have been exposed, and when belief in the absolute integrity of the police force has been shattered, we are more sceptical about such confessions. But when Ludo's book appeared in 1961 the situation was very different. Luckily for Ludo, an important book on the subject of brainwashing, *Battle for the Mind*, by the psychiatrist Dr William Sargant, a man who pioneered the use of drugs in the treatment of mental illness, had recently been published. In the course of a long and learned survey of various forms of brainwashing that had been practised by political and religious groups Sargant had devoted several pages to Evans and the reasons for his confession – his poor mental condition, fatigue and fear of physical violence from his interrogators.[21]

All this was supposition as no one aside from Evans, Jennings and Black has ever known what went on at Notting Hill Gate police station that night. But from a number of clues Ludo was at least able to show – if not definitively prove – that the police's timing of events was almost certainly a fabrication. According to Jennings, Evans's long and detailed confession had been volunteered – not in response to questioning – between 10 and 11.15 p.m., though he later told his mother, Mrs Probert, that the police had kept him up 'till 5 o'clock in the morning', a statement that was confirmed by at least two press reports in the *News Chronicle* and the *Evening Standard* the following day, both of which were headlined 'Man all Night with the Police'.

Ludo laboured under considerable constraints when analysing and seeking to explain the confession,

---

[21] Since Sargant's book was published in 1957, his theories have been confirmed by any number of witnesses, including victims of communist and fascist regimes, and those who have been beguiled by pseudo-religious cults. For example, Jenna Miscavige Hill (in her book *Beyond Belief*), niece of the director of the so-called Church of Scientology, on being grilled for a 'security check': 'At first you would know the answer, but as they asked the same question over and over again, with increasing levels of intensity suddenly you'd start to doubt yourself. These were confessions for things that you knew for a fact had never happened, and yet after hearing the same question for long enough, you'd start to think that maybe your answer was wrong . . . So many times I'd end a session not having done any of the things I'd admitted to, just because it was the only way to make it end.'

in particular when it came to criticising the police. At the time he wrote *Ten Rillington Place* there was still a widespread belief in the incorruptibility of the British police force – a belief which Ludo himself partly shared – and the idea that they might resort to force, or threats of force, to get a confession was regarded as almost incredible. Referring to Evans's fears that he would be beaten up, the lawyer Michael Eddowes said in his book on the case that Evans '*wrongly believed* that this might happen'.[22] Even William Sargant, when seeking to explain how Evans had been brainwashed into making a confession, dismissed Evans's suggestion – made later when he tried to backtrack – that he had been scared that the police would 'take me downstairs and knock me about' unless he confessed. 'Actually this could not happen to a man due to appear in a British court,' Sargant wrote, 'if only because expert defence lawyers would bring the matter up in court to show that the confession was made under duress.'[23]

So, even if British police officers betrayed their calling, British lawyers would see to it that justice would be done. Such sentiments, then widely held, made it very difficult for Ludo to make his case against Jennings and Black, who would almost certainly win any libel proceedings if they chose to challenge him. And even if

---

[22] Michael Eddowes, *The Man on Your Conscience* (emphasis added).

[23] William Sargant, *Battle for the Mind*.

he himself were prepared to take the risk, it was highly unlikely that his publishers, who would have to bear all the costs, would support him.

Ludo, as always, bent over backwards to see things from the police's point of view, writing:

> Do not let us forget that on that very morning Jennings had seen with his own eyes the pathetic little bundle that was Geraldine lying behind the washhouse door with a man's tie squeezed tightly round her neck. It must have been a sickening sight and Jennings would have been less than human not to have felt anger and disgust towards the person who he in all good faith believed was responsible for such an outrage.[24]

But this did not excuse their behaviour. In the classic formula beloved by publishers and libel lawyers, Ludo put on record that 'there has never been any suggestion and there is none now that either of them did anything improper', but this proviso did not altogether tally with what he went on to write. Apart from the deception about the time taken, Evans's statement, supposedly made quite voluntarily and in his own words, contained a number of expressions that would have been foreign to a man of his limited intelligence and education. For

---

[24] This and all subsequent Ludo quotes relating to the Evans case are from *Ten Rillington Place* unless otherwise stated.

example, he stated in his preliminary confession that his wife Beryl 'was incurring one debt after another' and used expressions such as 'no fixed abode' and 'under false pretences'. And the confession itself contained a variety of improbable statements and omissions. There was no explanation as to why Evans had strangled his child (a question that never bothered the learned judges who considered his evidence) and no description of how he – the 'tiny little chap', as described by Ludo – had managed to carry his wife's 107-pound body down the stairs in the middle of the night without somehow disturbing the Christies.

But it was in the days following the signing of the confession that, in Ludo's carefully chosen words, 'a more disturbing note creeps into the proceedings'. For it was when the police later began to prepare the case for the prosecution that they came up against a major difficulty that they had failed to foresee. Evans had stated – voluntarily, according to the police – that he had put the bodies of his wife and child in the washhouse on 8 and 10 November, respectively. Yet, throughout this period, workmen repairing the property had been continually in and out of 10 Rillington Place, using the disused washhouse at the rear as a place in which to store their tools and equipment overnight. It would have been impossible for them not to have noticed the presence of two bundled-up bodies in this very confined space, and all four workmen were adamant that the bodies had not been there by the time they left on 11 November and made statements to the police to that effect. What is more, they had worksheets to prove their movements on the relevant dates.

When first starting his research, Ludo had applied to the Director of Public Prosecutions to request access to all the papers concerning the case. He had expected this application to be refused, as had happened when Michael Eddowes made a similar application. Rather to his surprise, however, he was given not only the transcript of the trial but all the witness statements, including those of the workmen. Surprisingly there were two separate batches of statements. In the first batch the workmen stated quite categorically that the bodies could not have been in the washhouse on the dates named by Evans. The second batch however, made two days later, suggested that there might have been bodies but that the workmen had not noticed them. Ludo, who had personally inspected the washhouse and found it to be the size of an ordinary lavatory, knew this to be nonsense. So what had happened to make the workmen change their minds?

Ludo managed to track down one of the workers, a plasterer by the name of Mr Frederick Willis, who told him what had occurred after they had made their initial statements to the effect that the washhouse was empty on the relevant days:

When we got back to the house after our dinner, there was a black police car waiting outside. The driver said he'd come to fetch us to the police station for more questioning. We said we'd told them everything we knew already and he said 'What you said before doesn't quite fit in with the chief inspector's calculation.' They kept us waiting at the station about three hours and then they started shouting at us that we were wrong to say there were no bodies in the washhouse, they had thirty or forty witnesses to say there were. Well, we all stuck out for a time saying it was they who are wrong not us, but in the end – it must have been about five hours after we'd been there – we were all so browned off and exhausted, we were ready to sign anything and I remember our foreman saying 'Well if the police say there were bodies there, they must be right.'[25]

Claude Pain's deposition and notebook in the Craig/Bentley case 'disappeared'. So did the worksheets which proved that Mr Willis and his colleagues were in the washhouse after Evans had put the bodies there, according to his signed confession. And exactly the same thing had happened in the case of Richard Hauptmann, where a crucial worksheet had again gone missing (see page 174).

---

[25] *On My Way to the Club*. (The version of this interview that appears in *Ten Rillington Place* significantly omits the detail that the police shouted at the workmen.)

The evidence of the altered statements by the workmen, casting serious doubts on the validity of Evans's
confession, was never referred to in the subsequent trial
and was never even seen by his lawyers. But it pro-
foundly shocked Ludo when he found it in the file. For
the first time, he was faced with the indisputable fact
that the police were prepared to alter evidence when it
did not conform with their convictions. Writing about
it later,[26] when the possibility of libel no longer applied,
he withdrew his previous assertion that Jennings and
Black had done 'nothing improper'. They had, he now
wrote, perverted the course of justice and by rights
should have been prosecuted. But he still insisted, probably correctly, that they were convinced and remained
throughout convinced that Evans was guilty and were
thus able to convince themselves that Willis and his colleagues must have been mistaken about those dates. It
was Dr Sargant's view that in the process of extracting
a confession the interrogator ends up believing it just
as firmly as the man who 'confesses'. It was a sign of
Ludo's magnanimity that even in 2002 he could write
of Jennings and Black: 'They would have been less than
human if they had not felt not only disgust and anger
towards the perpetrator of such a double crime but also
a desire to bring him to justice. And in their view which
I would submit would have been the same as most of

---

[26] *Thirty-six Murders and Two Immoral Earnings.*

us, it was clear as crystal that the only credible perpetrator was Timothy John Evans.'[27]

We do not know how Jennings and Black coped with the subsequent unmasking of Christie as a mass murderer and the probability that they had sent an innocent man to the gallows. They had to live, too, with the knowledge that by failing to identify Christie as the killer they had allowed him to remain at large and commit further murders. Christie was to claim four more victims (including his own wife) before he was finally exposed and arrested. For two years following Evans's execution, his health deteriorated – due, according to Ludo, to anxiety – but in December 1952 his murderous urges revived and he strangled his wife for no better reason than that her presence in the house was an obstacle to his luring more victims there. He buried her under the floorboards in the front room, and shortly afterwards murdered three prostitutes – Hectorina McLennan, Kathleen Maloney and Rita Nelson – within weeks of one another. But he was losing touch with reality and the need to protect himself. In March 1953 he let out his flat and booked into a hotel, spending his days wandering aimlessly through the streets of London. Inevitably, the new tenant at 10 Rillington Place soon discovered one of the corpses, the police were called, and eventually all six

---

[27] *Thirty-six Murders and Two Immoral Earnings.*

victims were unearthed. The result was a media frenzy and overnight Christie was transformed into one of the world's foremost villains. His subsequent trial at the Old Bailey became a compulsive spectacle. Ludo wrote that 'the public and private benches were packed with people of fame in the legal, literary, political and social worlds all anxious to see for themselves this monster of modern times.' (They included the playwright Terence Rattigan, author of *The Winslow Boy*, reporting for the *Sunday Times*.)

Christie confessed to all the murders except for Geraldine's. (Ludo argued that the serial killer could find no extenuating circumstances for his murder of the baby, so refused to acknowledge it.) He was found guilty – with the jury rejecting his defence of insanity – and hanged on 15 July 1953.

The gruesome details of Christie's murders over-shadowed the earlier trial of Evans, which at the time had attracted little or no interest in the press. But to a small group of journalists and (mainly Labour) MPs, the implications were obvious: an innocent man had been executed, and a blow dealt to the reputation of British justice and the case for capital punishment, already under fire since the Craig/Bentley case of the previous year. These implications were not lost on the Home Secretary, Sir David Maxwell Fyfe, who had himself stated in the House of Commons in 1948: 'There is no possibility of an innocent man being hanged in this country and anyone who thinks there is, is living in a world of fantasy.'[28] With Christie still alive, albeit in the condemned cell, Maxwell Fyfe appointed a little-known barrister, J. Scott Henderson, to chair an inquiry into the Evans case prior to Christie's execution as a matter of urgency. Scott Henderson, a former civil servant who had worked in the Ministry of Health, was a veteran of the First World War's disastrous Gallipoli campaign, in which he served as a sergeant major in the Royal Dublin Fusiliers. Admitted to the Bar in 1927, his previous principal distinction had been to chair the Committee on Cruelty to Wild Animals and Humane Trap Awards Panel, which had recommended, *inter alia*, the abolition of the gin trap and greater protection for seals. Like many lawyers, he had difficulty in making his meaning clear, even when setting out his objective:

> The crucial question I have asked myself during my investigation is: Is there any doubt that Evans murdered his wife? Putting the question in the converse way, I have considered whether there is any possibility that Christie murdered Mrs Evans. But a negative answer to that last question does not necessarily mean that the answer to the first question is 'no'. On the other hand, I cannot be satisfied that the answer to the first question is 'no' unless

---

[28] Hansard.

I am also satisfied that the answer to the second question is that there is no possibility that Christie murdered Mrs Evans.[29]

Scott Henderson was tying himself up in knots, his difficulty being that Christie had by now confessed to killing Beryl, both at his trial and subsequently to Scott Henderson himself, though he altered the narrative by claiming that his victim was suicidal and that she actually encouraged him to have sex with her. The discrepancies were enough for Henderson to conclude that Christie's confession was 'not only unreliable but untrue'.

So the law that had convicted Evans on the basis of a false confession that it pronounced to be true now reaffirmed his guilt on the basis of a true confession that it pronounced to be false.

As a one-time sergeant major, Scott Henderson had done what Maxwell Fyfe had hoped he would do – namely, confirm that justice had been done in the case of Timothy Evans. This verdict, the Home Secretary insisted, showed that Henderson was no mere stooge of the Establishment (as his critics maintained) but a courageous investigator who was prepared to pursue the truth regardless of the consequences. Maxwell Fyfe proclaimed: 'I say that it will be a poor day for Great Britain when we cannot find men in this country who are

---

[29] Scott Henderson report.

prepared to undertake an enquiry and come fearlessly to the conclusion to which the facts point without any regard for the consequences of opinion.'[30] But this stirring tribute failed to silence those MPs who had made a careful study of Scott Henderson's report. Michael Foot denounced it as 'not worth the paper it was printed on', while Reginald Paget QC maintained 'we are attacking this report not because it is mistaken but because it is dishonest.'[31]

Lawyers have a wonderful way of ignoring those points that strike the layman as crucially important. Even so, it was a lawyer, the left-wing MP Geoffrey Bing QC, who did more than just pick holes in Scott Henderson's report and instead raised the most obvious question. If Evans were guilty, he said, then we had to accept the fantastic coincidence that in one small house in Notting Hill there lived at the same time two men who happened to be murdering people in exactly the same way. Ludo commented:

> He might have added that both of them murdered only women, both of them murdered only by strangling, both of them strangled with a ligature, both of them murdered women who were pregnant, both of them murdered women with no knickers on, both of them murdered

---

[30] Hansard.

[31] Hansard.

women who were found in dark blankets, both of them had intercourse with their victims at the time of death, both of them put the bodies of their victims in the washhouse, both doubled up the bodies of their victims, both moved their victims about the house, both sold their furniture before running away, both sold their furniture to the same dealer, both had newspaper cuttings of murder cases and both sold their dead wives' wedding rings. *Furthermore neither had any idea what the other was doing . . .*

Ludo loved to take ludicrous legal arguments to their logical extremes, though in this instance, while listing those points that Mr Bing might have added, he himself might have added that Michael Eddowes – who sparked his original interest in the story – had made an almost identical list in his own book.

Maxwell Fyfe was so concerned by the criticism of Scott Henderson that he asked him to produce a supplementary report dealing with the MPs' objections. Henderson complied but, though spending a great deal of time answering points raised about, for example, the workmen's evidence concerning the washhouse, failed to even mention the elephant in the room – the 'fantastic coincidence' of two stranglers living in one small house unbeknownst to one another.

Ludo ended his book with the second Scott Henderson report. He had already described its predecessor as 'one of the most extraordinary legal documents of the twentieth century – in its errors of omission and commission little short of a shambles'. It was the kind of comment that caused acute distress to a distinguished lawyer like Norman Birkett, who, though a friend and supporter of Ludo, could not refrain from rebuking him in the tones of an outraged schoolmaster: 'Mr Kennedy's language on the subject of this inquiry [Scott Henderson] is at times quite intemperate . . . this is to be regretted.' But such distaste, typical of many lawyers faced with criticism of fellow members of their profession, could not dispel Birkett's overall enthusiasm for Ludo's book:

It is the brilliant way in which this complicated and controversial story is told that makes it one of the most engrossing and fascinating books of its kind. As a work of fiction it would have been hailed as a great crime story: as a transcript from real life it holds the reader under a kind of spell. The story has nothing of splendour or nobility to commend it, and yet, as an example of human nature under the microscope, this book, once taken up, cannot easily be put down.[32]

The success of *Ten Rillington Place* ensured that Scott Henderson was not to be the last word on the subject and the book itself now became an important

---

[32] *Observer*, 15 January 1961.

element in the continuing story. One reason for its great success – it remained in print for nearly thirty years and in 1971 was made into a film starring Richard Attenborough as Christie and John Hurt as Evans – was the author's confidence in his narrative. Some years earlier, in *One Man's Meat*, Ludo had considered the situation of the biographer faced with a number of possible answers for a particular question. 'What is the biographer to do? If he is a scholar he will set down all the possibilities, arrive at no conclusions and leave the reader dissatisfied. But if he is an artist he will sift all the evidence carefully, allow it to lead him to the most likely conclusions, and set down those conclusions with all the weight and persuasion his art can bring to bear.' Applying this rule to the story of Evans and Christie meant examining all the transcripts and reports, and where there was no written evidence – as with Evans's grilling by the police at Notting Hill Gate – coming to a definite conclusion about what had happened. Nowhere in his narrative does Ludo act like a judge summing up and posing alternative conclusions – 'You may think this . . . you may think that' – leaving the readers to decide for themselves.

One of the differences between the lawyer and the layman when judging guilt or innocence is that the latter will almost always ask whether the man in the dock is the sort of person who is likely to have committed the crime for which he is on trial. The lawyer, on the other hand, is only concerned with the question: did this particular person do this particular thing? Other issues are irrelevant. One reason why Ludo's account is so convincing is that, while examining all the evidence as carefully as any lawyer would, he writes as a novelist (or artist) for whom the characters and life-histories of Evans and Christie are all-important. With Christie, this was difficult, as even a top-grade psychiatrist might find it hard to explain his actions. But Ludo's account of Evans – a man caught up in events he could not understand, who by his own lies and evasions brought about his own death – is wholly convincing, making the arguments about particular pieces of evidence seem irrelevant.

Apart from the author's narrative skills and his mastery of language, his book's impact was all the more effective in that it was not written as anti-capital punishment propaganda. Ludo made this clear in a brief 'author's note' at the opening:

There are several things which this book is not. It is not, primarily, an attack on capital punishment. It is not an attack on the British legal system, which despite occasional human failings is one of the fairest in the world, it is not an attack on the integrity of the British police who have a difficult job to do and on the whole do it extraordinarily well . . . What the book is, is the story of two men; the one an ex-police officer who became a

necrophilic strangler; the other a 25-year-old youth with
a ten-and-a-half-year-old brain, *and of the unique and
terrible thing that happened to him.*[33]

The unintended consequence of this approach was
that the book became a much more powerful argument against capital punishment than it would have
been if Ludo had used it as a platform for a political
campaign.

In 1960, prior to publication, Ludo sent a copy of
Ten Rillington Place to R. A. Butler, who had succeeded
Maxwell Fyfe as Home Secretary, urging him to set up
a new inquiry into the case. Butler never thanked Ludo
for the book, nor even replied. However, two months
after publication and in response to widespread publicity for the text, the Tory government announced that
there would be a debate in the House of Commons.
Several Labour MPs made powerful appeals for a new
inquiry, but Butler rejected all of them, claiming that he
had read *Ten Rillington Place* and so could say that it
contained no new evidence. 'I had always thought
R. A. Butler a rather flabby individual,' Ludo wrote
later, after insisting that the Home Secretary had obviously not read his book, 'and in his reply for the
government he was at his flabbiest.'[34]

---

[33] Emphasis added.

[34] *On My Way to the Club.*

Calls for a new inquiry had been led by the Shadow Home Secretary, the Labour Party's Frank Soskice, who pronounced solemnly: 'I believe that if ever there was a debt due to justice and the reputation both of our own judicial system and the public conscience, that is one that the Home Secretary should now pay.'[35] Three years later, in 1964, when Harold Wilson's Labour Party came to power and Soskice was made Home Secretary, hopes were raised that at last something would be done. By then, though, Soskice had had an extraordinary change of heart: 'I really do not think that an enquiry would serve any useful purpose,'[36] he announced. He was, however, eventually forced to change his mind yet again following continued campaigning, notably by Harold Evans, then editor of the *Northern Echo* (and later editor of the *Sunday Times* and *The Times*). A Timothy Evans Committee was formed, which included Ludo, Evans and Michael Eddowes, and 113 MPs signed a motion calling for an inquiry. Soskice thereupon caved in and appointed a young High Court judge, Sir Daniel Brabin, to investigate the case. Brabin spent two months at the law courts interviewing seventy-nine witnesses, including Ludo, and at the end of it all came to the conclusion that though Evans had probably not murdered Geraldine (the crime for which he had been

---

[35] Hansard.

[36] Hansard.

hanged), he probably *had* murdered Beryl. Brabin thus confirmed the extraordinary story that there had been two stranglers living in the same little house in Notting Hill, unbeknownst to one another.

All the same, Brabin had to conclude that no jury would have convicted Evans of either murder had all the evidence been made known to them. This was enough for the new Home Secretary, Roy Jenkins, to grant Evans a free pardon on 18 October 1966, four days after publication of the Brabin report and sixteen years after Evans's execution.

The strange and alarming thing is how many people were happy to accept Brabin's verdict – proof, perhaps, of a deep and widespread reluctance to acknowledge that an innocent man had been hanged with the full approval of the political and judicial Establishments. And there was no shortage of writers and journalists eager to endorse the official view. One, John Newton Chance, a prolific writer of science fiction, wrote a book, *The Crimes at Rillington Place,* in which he insisted on Evans's guilt. Chance was supported by the *Sunday Express* columnist Robert Pitman, a favourite of his proprietor Lord Beaverbrook. And a similar line was taken by another crime writer, Rupert Furneaux, who had reached the same conclusion as Brabin in his book *The Two Stranglers of Rillington Place*, which was published long before the Brabin report, in 1961.

More surprising was the appearance many years later of yet another such book, proof that the two stranglers theory was still alive and kicking. *The Two Killers of Rillington Place* (1994) painted Timothy Evans as a violent psychopath who killed his wife in a fit of rage and later strangled his baby because she was crying. Along the way, Ludo was subjected to a fusillade of abuse – he was a liar and a fantasist who deliberately omitted vital pieces of evidence that were at variance with his viewpoint. Scott Henderson, on the other hand, was 'a man for whom the phrase *sans peur et sans reproche* might have been coined, a man of infinitely superior record to Kennedy'.[37]

The extraordinary thing about the book was that its author, John Eddowes, was the son of Michael Eddowes, the solicitor whose book *The Man on Your Conscience* had originally awakened Ludo's interest in the Rillington Place story. Critics noted the rather surprising fact that Eddowes made no mention of his father's earlier work or the fact that he took completely the opposite approach so, in response, when his book was published in paperback, he added what must be one of the most bizarre introductions to a book ever to be published: 'I left Michael [his father] out,' he wrote, 'because he was too mad, and his work on the case too embarrassing, to be suitably included . . . Everybody

---

[37] John Eddowes, *The Two Killers of Rillington Place*.

who knew Michael well agreed that he was mentally ill, a fantasist and a liar.' John Eddowes had done his best, he said, to help his poor father – 'putting him in a home to undergo electro-convulsive therapy' – but all to no avail.

To anyone familiar with Michael Eddowes's sober if poorly written book, such condemnation would hardly recommend its author as a level-headed enquirer after truth. As for Ludo, with whom I corresponded about *The Two Killers of Rillington Place* in 2001, he explained:

> I owe a great debt of gratitude to John Eddowes as it was entirely through him that I secured what every writer dreams of securing – a five-figure tax-free sum . . . He had to decide, he said, whether my conclusions (also his dad's) were 'flawed' or a 'fraud' and came down firmly on the view that I was a fraud, so with the help of Goodman Derrick & Co I got his publishers to pay up.

Though delighted with his tax-free gains, Ludo may well have been depressed by the ease with which John Eddowes had found a publisher for a book that was taken seriously by some critics and was so successful that it was reprinted as a paperback. Thirty or so years after Evans had received a pardon the idea that he had after all been guilty could still find acceptance. This was no doubt partly due to the legal confusion in which the case had ended. Evans had been found guilty only of the murder of his baby, for which he had been pardoned. But this left open the possibility that he had murdered his wife, as Sir Daniel Brabin had concluded. And Brabin's report had followed the publication of *Ten Rillington Place*; only in later editions and in his memoirs was Ludo able to refer to it.

On more general grounds, the survival of the two-stranglers-in-one-house theory seems to point to a reluctance on the part of the public – not just a handful of right-wing journalists – to accept that the police, the courts and the political authorities could make a terrible mistake. And that reluctance stemmed not from a wish to conform to the decisions of the powers that be and preserve the faith in our wonderful British justice, but from the lurking fear that what happened to Evans (his conviction, if not his execution, given that capital punishment was abolished in 1965) might happen to any one of us, a fear that had, at all costs, to be suppressed.

Ludo was to discover that Timothy Evans was by no means an isolated case.

Chapter 2

'The Amazing Case of Patrick Meehan'

In 1966 Ludo and Moira decided to sell their house at Amersham in Buckinghamshire, and move to Makerstoun, Roxburghshire, about forty miles south of Edinburgh. Moira, who had given up dancing and the stage to devote herself to her husband and two small children, needed little persuasion as she herself was Scottish. As for Ludo, he was drawn back to the country of his birth not just by childhood memories but even more so by his love, inherited from his father, of outdoor pursuits – hunting, shooting and fishing – sports for which there were only limited facilities in rural Bucks.

Anyone who reads Ludo's books will, from time to time, be reminded of Richard Hannay, the hero of John Buchan's *The Thirty-Nine Steps* and other yarns – the dashing, good-looking, upper-class gent who loves to escape the trials and tribulations of life by tramping across the heather with a rifle or standing knee-high in some Highland burn in the hope of catching a wily trout or salmon. 'I have always loved working with pointers,' Ludo wrote in a typically Buchanish passage in his memoirs. 'Trained to lope up and down the line, never more than gunshot range ahead, they sniff continuously about them, when the sniff is positive, they freeze as if to stone . . . It was not a grand shoot. If at the end of a long day's walking we had killed a dozen grouse, we felt we had done well. On return to the lodge there would be hot baths and whisky.'[38]

There was a Buchanesque air, too, about Ludo's neighbours – rich, landowning, fellow Old Etonians, such as Lord 'Johnnie' Dalkeith, Lord 'Dawick' Haig, Robin McEwan and the Laird of Marchmont. These members of Scotland's upper class, many of them inter-related, all knew each other and took part in the same social engagements. Thus it was inevitable that sooner or later Ludo and Moira would come across a dashing Edinburgh lawyer whose sister-in-law was one of their neighbours.

'Nicky' Fairbairn, younger than Ludo by fourteen years but with many common characteristics, was a flamboyant, devil-may-care character who listed 'making love' as one of his recreations in *Who's Who*. Like Ludo, he had been neglected by his mother and had doted on his father, a distinguished Edinburgh

---

[38] *On My Way to the Club*.

psychoanalyst. Educated at Loretto and Edinburgh University, he made a brief, unsuccessful attempt to follow in his father's footsteps as a doctor before turning to the law. He was admitted to the Scottish Bar at the age of twenty-three, and after a number of false starts established himself as a leading criminal defence lawyer in Glasgow, most often working in conjunction with an outstanding solicitor named Joe Beltrami, a man with long experience in the courts and invaluable knowledge of the city's underworld. Beltrami was proud of the fact that the pair 'never lost a client to the hangman',[39] despite representing a number of them in capital cases over the course of more than a decade. Thanks, in part, to his association with Beltrami, Fairbairn prospered, acquiring a rich and aristocratic wife and a tumbledown castle with a private chapel at Fordell in Fife. A conspicuous figure at the law courts with his wing collar, tartan trousers, fancy waistcoats and silver-tipped cane, he was also politically ambitious – he became a Tory MP in 1974 and Solicitor General for Scotland in 1979. But Fairbairn was too flamboyant for the world of politics. He took to drink, blotted his copybook, divorced, and died prematurely in 1995 aged only sixty-one. (His entertaining memoir, published in 1987, bore the somewhat prophetic title *A Life is too Short*.)

---

[39] This and all subsequent quotes attributed to Joe Beltrami are from *A Deadly Innocence*.

Fairbairn first met Ludo in November 1968 at a lunch party given by Mrs Auriole Butler, a lady he describes as 'a noble woman who always had the best roast beef and the most virile butlers'.[40] As it happened, it was Ludo's forty-ninth birthday, and Fairbairn, a skilled amateur painter who also fancied himself as a poet, penned some verses in his honour, which he sang to the tune of 'Clementine':

> Oh my handsome, oh my brilliant
> Oh my Ludo, so sublime
> Are they gone and lost forever
> Are your powers all past their prime?
>
> Oh my handsome, oh my brilliant
> Oh my Ludo, so divine
> Have you really gone for ever
> Promise fails at forty-nine.
>
> You're a genius, you're a wonder
> Casanova in your time
> What a shame then that already
> You have gone into decline.[41]

If Fairbairn believed there was truth in his mocking verses, he could not possibly have foreseen that he would be instrumental in dragging a reluctant Ludo

---

[40] *A Life Too Short.*

[41] *A Life Too Short.*

back to what he was best at – the exposure of injustice. By chance (and Ludo always insisted that the course of his life was dictated by a succession of chances), he met Fairbairn again the following year, when they were both speakers at a Glasgow University debate. Afterwards they caught the last train back to Edinburgh together and Fairbairn made the startling announcement that the very next day he would be making a closing speech on behalf of a man accused of murder, whom he knew to be innocent.

Three months previously, in July 1969, Fairbairn explained, two men had broken into the seaside home in Ayr of a Jewish bingo-hall owner named Abraham Ross. After restraining Ross and his wife Rachel, the pair stole several thousand pounds in cash and traveller's cheques from the safe before making their escape. The couple's cries for help went unheard and they remained tied up over the weekend. They were finally discovered on the Monday and were taken to hospital. Mrs Ross, aged seventy-two, who had been sprayed with ammonia, subsequently died in hospital. Mr Ross, who had suffered head injuries in the assault, was unable to tell the police much about their attackers, who had worn masks, other than that they both had Glasgow accents and referred to one another as 'Pat' and 'Jim'.

Fairbairn's client, referred to him by Joe Beltrami, was Patrick (Paddy) Meehan, then aged forty-two, a convicted criminal from the Gorbals who specialised in safe-blowing, but who, significantly, had no record of crimes of violence. A clever, determined character, though never a very successful crook, he impressed Fairbairn and all the lawyers who later acted for him with his obsessive attention to detail, even if it was hard to like the man. 'How much simpler life would be,' the historian A. J. P. Taylor once wrote, 'if the victims of injustice were attractive characters.'[42] Perhaps he was thinking of Alfred Dreyfus, but he would no doubt have felt the same about Paddy Meehan. 'He was not a likeable person,' Joe Beltrami remembered, 'particularly when matters were not going his way. He was inconsiderate of others and selfish. I was to find that he had a nasty streak in him.' Another solicitor, Leonard Murray, who later acted for Meehan, described him even more vehemently as 'one of the most unpleasant characters I have known'.[43] Nicholas Fairbairn wrote in similar terms. Yet the surprising fact is that all these men were convinced that Meehan was innocent and, just as surprising, that they were prepared to work for his release without receiving a penny for their pains. (Meehan's wife Betty no doubt played her part in retaining the loyalty of the lawyers as she – in marked contrast to her husband – commanded their respect and admiration.)

---

[42] R. Ingrams, *Quips and Quotes*, 2013.

[43] Conversation with the author.

It was Meehan's misfortune that he had been in Stranraer, fifty miles south of Ayr, on the night in question in the company of another criminal, James Griffiths. Born in Rochdale in 1935, Griffiths had been in trouble all his life, with a string of convictions for robbery and GBH, and, unlike Meehan, possessed a number of firearms. (It was typical of Ludo, with his natural inclination to see the good in everyone, that he recorded that Griffiths liked to listen to Beethoven and Tchaikovsky while Meehan was a 'regular blood donor'.[44])

On the night of the break-in, Meehan and Griffiths had travelled to Stranraer to stake out the council offices, in particular the motor taxation office, in the hope of stealing unused logbooks that they needed for the resale of stolen cars – car-theft being a speciality of both men. But it proved to be a fruitless expedition. The council offices turned out to be overlooked by several new houses, and after inspecting some cars at a tourist hotel in the hope of stealing valuables, they reluctantly decided to drive back to Glasgow empty-handed, arriving home at about 5 p.m.

The break-in at Ayr and the subsequent death of Mrs Ross provoked a public outcry and, as always when the media gives front-page coverage to a particular

---

[44] This and all subsequent Ludo quotes relating to the Meehan case are from *A Presumption of Innocence*.

crime, the police felt under unusual pressure to make arrests. Given that Mr Ross was unable to help very much beyond saying that his two assailants called one another Pat and Jim, the inspectors who were assigned to the case were relieved and delighted when, during a routine investigation of known Glasgow criminals, they took a statement from (Pat) Meehan in which he described his trip with (Jim) Griffiths to Stranraer. (Of course, Meehan omitted any incriminating details about their intention to steal logbooks.) Eight days after the death of Mrs Ross, Meehan was flabbergasted when he was arrested and charged with her murder, the assault of her husband and the theft of £1,800 and some traveller's cheques.

Indignant and incredulous, Meehan remained convinced that his innocence was bound to become clear sooner or later. His only problem was with Griffiths, who, prior to the Ayr murder, was already wanted by the police and had no wish to identify himself, let alone tell the police of his whereabouts. In desperation, Meehan, convinced that he needed Griffiths to back up his alibi, then gave away his address to the police. It was a fatal move. A posse of five CID officers descended on 14 Holyrood Crescent, where Griffiths was hiding in an upstairs flat. When the police kicked in the door, Griffiths responded with a shotgun, injuring one of the officers, all of whom were unarmed. As they retreated, he started firing indiscriminately at people in the street and in the houses opposite. When police marksmen arrived, Griffiths fled via the back garden, commandeered a car, injuring its owner, crashed the car, then strode into a pub, firing at the ceiling and shouting, 'I'll shoot anyone who moves. I've already shot four policemen.' After a further chase and more shooting, Griffiths was eventually cornered in a cul-de-sac and shot dead by a police marksman. In the space of ninety minutes, Joe Beltrami recorded, 'he had killed a man, wounded five detectives and injured eleven civilians'.

'You'll need to get him,' Meehan had previously told Beltrami, 'I need him to clear me.' But he was wrong. Griffiths might well have confirmed Meehan's story, but that did not prove that it was true. And now, as a result of his crazy suicidal behaviour, Griffiths had, in the eyes of the police and the public, simply confirmed his guilt. Beltrami himself was of the same mind. 'I remember thinking that if Griffiths were innocent, as Meehan so securely stated, why on earth should he virtually commit suicide?'[45] The authorities were so certain of the matter that the Crown Office issued an unprecedented statement: 'With the death of Griffiths and the apprehension of Patrick Meehan, the police are no longer looking for any other person suspected of implication in the incident concerning Mr and Mrs

---

[45] The answer to this question would become apparent after the trial, when Fairbairn obtained a recording of Griffiths talking on a BBC programme. See page 77.

Ross at Ayr.' Fairbairn and Beltrami were naturally outraged, but it is easy to see why the police were so confident, particularly in view of Mr Ross's statement about 'Pat' and 'Jim'. Surely the likelihood of two sets of Pat and Jim being at large on the night in question was unbelievable. It was to remain a coincidence too great, even, for a time, for Ludo to accept.

Fairbairn and Beltrami, however, convinced by Meehan of his innocence, were confident that they could obtain, if not a Not Guilty verdict, a Not Proven one – a Scottish variation meaning that the jury finds the charges neither proved nor disproved. Despite 'Pat and Jim', there seemed to be just too many difficulties for the prosecution to overcome. Abraham Ross was adamant that 'Pat and Jim' both spoke with Glasgow accents. But Jim Griffiths was an Englishman from Rochdale with a Lancashire accent. Again, Ross stated that when the two men finally left his bungalow, it was daylight. Yet there were witnesses, including two teenage girls who Meehan and Griffiths had given a lift to on their way home, who would swear that the two men were miles away from Ayr when it was still dark.

The difficulty facing the police was that their evidence was entirely circumstantial. There was nothing at all to link Meehan directly to the crime – no bloodstained clothes, no unexpectedly large payments into his bank account following the murder – simply the 'Pat and Jim' coincidence and Griffiths's suicidal rampage, which appeared to confirm his guilt. Given this absence of evidence, the police quite cynically decided to invent some, knowing full well that the prosecution lawyers – as turned out to be the case – would be reluctant to expose them and thereby damage the cherished 'integrity' of the police force. Although Abraham Ross had heard his attackers' voices, he had not seen their faces. An identity parade was therefore held and arranged in such a way that he would be given every bit of help and encouragement beforehand to identify Meehan. In addition, small pieces of paper were suddenly 'discovered' in a coat belonging to the dead Griffiths, which were shown to match pieces of paper taken from Mr Ross's safe, even though other officers had previously stated that the safe was completely empty after the robbery. From the police's point of view, this plan had the advantage that Griffiths was dead and therefore in no position to rebut the charge.

The case came to court towards the end of 1969, and things went against Meehan from the start. The prosecuting counsel, Ewan Stewart – nicknamed 'Napoleon' – was an outstanding advocate, but it was the judge, Lord Grant, who was the biggest obstacle from the point of view of Meehan and his lawyers, Beltrami, Fairbairn and Fairbairn's junior, John Smith (who would later become leader of the Labour Party). Sometimes referred to as 'Lord Grunt', Grant – who had recently come out of hospital after a serious throat operation – was in any case short-tempered. As a result, Fairbairn noted with customary prolixity 'of his generous and appropriate patronage of the national tope'.[46] He made it clear from the start that he believed Meehan was guilty. 'This court has to keep in mind,' he lectured Fairbairn early on in proceedings, 'not only the interests of the accused but the interests of the public. That has been laid down more than once recently, and it is possibly putting an end to a trend by judges in the past who tended to give greater weight to the accused's interests than was justified, to the detriment of the public itself and to the administration of justice.'[47] From then on his bias was clear and he missed no opportunity to belittle the defence, even at one point rounding on Fairbairn: 'Fairbairn, would you please not be more stupid than you really are.'

It is significant that Fairbairn and Beltrami, both of whom had experience of a number of murder trials, felt that there was something unique about this one. 'I had had many hot and searing exchanges over the years,' Fairbairn wrote, 'but in no other case and before no other court had I been the object of such a course of

---

[46] Nicholas Fairbairn, *A Life is too Short*. Somewhat more succinctly, another legal eminence once told me that Grant was 'a bottle-a-day man', while one Scottish lawyer remembered that he was 'fond of a good bucket'.

[47] This and all subsequent quotes involving or citing Fairbairn are from Nicholas Fairbairn, *A Life is too Short*.

deliberate obstruction as that to which I was subjected in the defence of Meehan.' Beltrami echoed this sentiment: 'There was a dreadful feeling in the courtroom – one that I have never experienced in the past and fortunately never have since. It seemed that anyone on Meehan's side was indeed on the wrong side of justice, law and order.'

The climax came with Grant's summing up (or 'charge', as it is called in the Scottish courts). He ignored the evidence of the two hitch-hiking girls and their boyfriends that it was dark when Meehan and Griffiths met up with them, and he argued that the two men could have spent just half an hour at the Rosses' bungalow, despite the fact that Mr Ross and the police had both stated that they had been there for 'several hours'.

Typical was the way he dealt with the difficulty of Mr Ross's testimony that both of his attackers spoke with Glaswegian accents when Jim Griffiths clearly did not:

As regards the evidence by Mr Ross that both assailants had Glasgow accents there is, of course, the difficulty that Jim Griffiths undoubtedly had an English voice. Well, there again you heard the argument pro and con from the Solicitor General and Mr Fairbairn on this matter, the possible explanations and so on and you will consider the matter as part of the whole evidence in the case and give it what weight you think fit.[48]

---

[48] *A Presumption of Innocence.*

So, faced with a major and apparently baffling discrepancy in the case against Meehan, instead of confronting it for what it was, Grant invited the jury to put it to one side while considering all of the evidence that pointed the other way – to Meehan's guilt.

Even more dishonest was the way the judge dealt with Griffiths's violent death, which to many, including the police, had looked like a suicidal act by a man determined to avoid arrest for the Ayr murder. 'Put those events from your minds,' Grant told the jury, having first put them there himself and knowing full well how difficult it would be to forget the sensational circumstances of Griffiths's end. He went on to remind the jury that Mr Ross had said that the two raiders helped themselves to whisky lemonade 'and Meehan drinks whisky lemonade'. Only then did he add, 'This does not get us very far', which begs the question of why he brought it up in the first place, especially since whisky lemonade was a very popular drink in Scotland at the time.

There was despondency on Meehan's side following Grant's summing-up. Beltrami described feeling 'ill-at-ease' as he waited for the jury's verdict and wrote that Meehan himself was downcast. When the foreman of the jury eventually announced a verdict of 'guilty by majority (nine out of fifteen)' and the judge sentenced Meehan to life imprisonment, he stood firmly to attention and addressed Lord Grant: 'I want to say this, sir, I'm innocent of this crime and so is Jim Griffiths.' Turning to the jury, Meehan continued, 'You have made a terrible mistake.' When Fairbairn, with Beltrami and Smith, visited him in the cells to console him, the lawyer was in tears, as was Beltrami.

Meehan appealed against his conviction and Fairbairn was hopeful that he would succeed, particularly as he had since obtained a recording of Griffiths giving an interview to a BBC religious programme about convicted prisoners, which proved that he had a Lancashire accent. Moreover, in the course of the interview, Griffiths said that he could not face a further term inside and that, if the police came for him again, he would shoot his way out. This demolished the prosecution's argument that his suicidal shoot-out was proof of his involvement in Mrs Ross's murder. And there was also the biased summing-up by Lord Grant. But the presiding Appeal Court justice, Lord Clyde, dismissed all the criticism of his fellow judge with what Fairbairn – who had a regrettable weakness for obscure and obsolete words[49] – called 'fribbling observations' and 'splenetic hypocrisy'. He rejected the notion of recalling Mr Ross to hear the recording of Griffiths, and at times made no effort to conceal his impatience, at one point leaning forward and addressing the defence team of Beltrami,

---

[49] Two pages of Fairbairn's memoir chosen at random include the following: agamist, apparitor, ebriosity, hispid, imparadised, potation and pithecoid.

Fairbairn and Smith with the words 'You've already had one trial, how many trials do you want – half a dozen?'[50]

The appeal was dismissed and Meehan was driven back to Barlinnie Prison, remarking to his four-man police escort, 'If there was still capital punishment they would take me out one morning soon and kill me.'[51] He might have added that one of the people he had to thank for the change was Ludovic Kennedy.[52]

There were always two strands to the Meehan story, but they were intertwined. One was the story of Meehan and Griffiths, Meehan's wrongful conviction and the long struggle to clear his name. The other was the story of the two men – Ian Waddell and William 'Tank' McGuiness – who were in fact responsible for the break-in and the murder of Mrs Ross. Both were hardened criminals, described by Beltrami as 'the odd couple'. Small and lean, McGuiness was a professional criminal and expert safe-blower, a man with psychopathic tendencies who inspired respect and even fear in his fellow crooks. By contrast, Waddell was boastful and garrulous – 'a drunk, loose-tongued and somewhat haggard', according to Beltrami. Ludo, who

---

[50] *A Life Too Short.*

[51] Patrick Meehan, *Innocent Villain.*

[52] Capital punishment had been abolished in 1965. Ludo's work in exposing the miscarriage of justice in the Timothy Evans case was highly influential in the abolition campaign.

came to know him quite well, was more charitable, calling him 'a man of cheerful disposition and indistinct speech'.

It was Meehan himself who first identified Ian Waddell (of whom at the time he knew nothing) as one of the guilty men. As it happened Waddell had been questioned earlier by the police about the Ayr murder but had provided himself with a convincing alibi. However, by a great stroke of fortune, while Meehan was on remand in Barlinnie, Waddell was awaiting trial in the same wing on charges relating to a separate offence. It did not take Meehan long to identify the 'loose-tongued' Waddell as one of the true perpetrators, if only because Waddell was plainly experiencing feelings of guilt about Meehan's arrest and talking quite openly about his role in the Ayr break-in and murder to fellow prisoners. Two of these men subsequently volunteered to give evidence for the defence at Meehan's trial. When Waddell was impeached as another witness for the defence, Lord Grant went out of his way to remind him more than once that he was not required to answer any of the questions if he thought that they might incriminate him. Unsurprisingly, for a time Waddell remained uncooperative and refused to answer Fairbairn, but then he dropped his guard. Asked if it was true that when he was summoned by police following the Ayr murder he had gone to a Glasgow solicitor named William Carlin and given him two hundred pounds in unused five-pound notes to accompany him to the station, Waddell denied the accusation emphatically. This worried Grant, who reminded Waddell that 'dealings between a solicitor and client are privileged'. In other words, he had no obligation to answer. Waddell however, for whatever reason, persisted with his denial. A little later, Carlin was called and confirmed the story about the two hundred pounds, before adding that Waddell had been concerned that he might be charged with murder. Nobody was able to explain how a man in Waddell's position had come by two hundred pounds or why he thought he might be charged with murder and was so concerned about it that he was prepared to part with what was, for him, a very large sum of money.

Following Meehan's conviction, Waddell was charged with perjury and given a three-year prison sentence, though in the event he served only two years. He was released in 1972 only to be rearrested shortly afterwards and convicted of being in possession of a loaded revolver. He was due to be defended by a colleague of Joe Beltrami, William Dunn, but Dunn was on holiday, so Beltrami offered his services, which Waddell was happy to accept, saying he had no objection to Beltrami simultaneously representing Meehan. At the time, the solicitor was preparing a dossier on Meehan's behalf for the Secretary of State for Scotland.

It was thanks to Waddell's wild and unpredictable behaviour that the Meehan story remained alive. But if

Meehan was helped by Waddell he was helped just as much by his wife Betty – 'a wife of exceptional courage and character', as Ludo described her. Betty Meehan took up the cudgels after her husband's appeal was thrown out. She had written to Ludo in April 1971, presumably on the suggestion of Nicholas Fairbairn, who knew of his interest in the case, pleading for his help:

I would appreciate it if you could do anything to bring all that happened into the open. As I say again, Paddy and Jim had never heard of Mr Ross until after this crime, and I know that if not this week or this year, he will clear himself some day. Meantime it's a living hell for all of us and we need all the help we can get to shorten the time he will be in prison.

'Such an appeal,' Ludo wrote, 'was not to be resisted.' Besides which, his curiosity, sparked initially by that chance conversation on a train with Nicholas Fairbairn, had been aroused. He obtained a seven-hundred-page transcript of the trial and visited Joe Beltrami at his Glasgow office, impressing the lawyer with the speed with which he mastered the details of the case. He also began what was to be an epic correspondence with Paddy Meehan and in the spring of 1971 visited him at the grim prison of Peterhead on the Aberdeenshire coast. Meehan, realising the importance of winning

Ludo over to his case, was on his best behaviour, and Ludo was impressed by the way he had preserved a sense of humour in spite of his situation.

Everything seemed to point to Meehan's innocence. All of his solicitors, headed by the patient and long-suffering Joe Beltrami, were convinced of it, as was the governor of Peterhead, Alexander Angus. But there was a snag – in Ludo's view a major one. Along with many of Meehan's sympathisers, he was still unable to accept the apparent coincidence of two sets of criminals called Pat and Jim, both at large in the same area of Scotland on the same night. Meehan himself had no way of convincing Ludo, apart from suggesting to him what he himself believed, namely that the police had fabricated the Pat and Jim story in order to bolster the case against him and Griffiths, which was otherwise very thin. With his knowledge of police tactics derived from the Craig/ Bentley case and the 10 Rillington Place saga, Ludo had no difficulty in accepting that explanation. Much would depend, however, on a telex message that the police had issued after the Rosses were discovered on the Monday after the break-in. It therefore came as a shock to Ludo (as well as Meehan) when the telex was finally made available to them showing that 'Pat' and 'Jim' were given as the names of the two wanted men – in other words long before Meehan and Griffiths became suspects. To his 'eternal shame', Ludo wrote later, the police's revelation about Pat and Jim left him with strong doubts about Meehan's innocence and therefore reluctant to commit himself to campaigning for his acquittal. He had many other assignments and had promised the Meehans to write not a book, but an article on their behalf for the *Scotsman*, but now, with his loss of certainty, even this article 'went into abeyance'.

But in the meantime the loose-tongued Waddell had been talking again, this time to Joe Beltrami in Barlinnie. He was anxious to help Meehan, he said, having got it into his head that if he told his story after taking a so-called 'truth drug', the evidence could not be used to put him on trial for murder. He had also got it into his head that he could make a large sum of money – as much as thirty thousand pounds, he hoped – from selling this drug-induced confession to the media. Beltrami accordingly contacted a BBC friend, David Roberts, to inform him of Waddell's scheme. As a result, two more BBC men, David Scott and Ken Vass, met Waddell upon his release. Both of them had tiny tape-recorders concealed in their ties.

Waddell was well aware that he was playing with fire, but the lure of the £30,000 fee for his story was too much for him. In extended, secretly recorded interviews with Scott and Vass he confessed to the Ayr murder, giving a detailed description of the Rosses' bungalow. The lounge, he said, had a highly polished floor; he had seen a luminous clock in the hallway;

and photographs of a young child were in the bottom
drawer of a cupboard they had ransacked. Mr Ross
confirmed all of these details in a subsequent interview
with the BBC. In a series of confessions made later to
various newspapers Waddell added yet more details to
his description, all of which were shown to be correct.
Asked about 'Pat and Jim', he said the names were
often used by criminals in situations such as the Ayr
raid when they wished to avoid giving away any clues
about their true identities.

All of this was more than enough to dispel any
remaining doubts. Ludo finally set about writing his
promised article for the *Scotsman*, which was published
under the headline 'Was Patrick Meehan Wrongly
Convicted?' on 14 December 1972.

Though still reluctant to write a book about the case,
Ludo was unable to resist the opportunity to pursue the
story in the company of David Roberts and Ken Vass,
both of whom were encouraging Waddell's faith in his
truth-drug experiment and £30,000 fee. Ludo liked
the idea of doing the truth-drug experiment in front of
the cameras, but was well aware that the BBC would
never cough up Waddell's anticipated thirty-thousand-
pound fee. Consequently, Ludo, Beltrami, Roberts and
Vass arranged a meeting with Waddell to discuss how
they might proceed. Unfortunately, Waddell failed to
show up (according to Beltrami he was drunk). Another
meeting was organised, but Ludo failed to get to grips

with Waddell and the meeting broke up in disarray. The BBC men, however, were not too concerned as they already had Waddell secretly recorded on tape confessing to everything.

Several months later, in July 1973, the BBC finally broadcast a programme on the Meehan case, complete with Waddell's confession. Thereafter, thanks in part to Ludo's well-publicised involvement, the rest of the media gradually began to take more of an interest in the story, and particularly in Waddell's repeated and detailed confessions. The authorities' continued reluctance to take any action against Waddell seemed to indicate that they were unwilling to look again at the conviction of Meehan for fear of what might be revealed.

The determination to do nothing in the hope that, in the end, Waddell would get bored, the media would lose interest and the campaigners would pack up and go home seemed to extend to Parliament, where questions were being asked of successive secretaries of state only to be brushed aside. In February 1974 Harold Wilson's Labour Party defeated Edward Heath's Conservatives in the General Election. Labour's William Ross returned as Secretary of State for Scotland in Harold Wilson's new government, reviving hopes that Meehan, who by now had been incarcerated for four years, might finally be released. Instead, Ross – an obdurate, unyielding character – again slammed the prison door in his face. He had come to the conclusion, he said, 'that there are no grounds that would justify the exercise of the Royal Prerogative of Mercy, or taking any other action in the case'.[53]

This perverse decision had one beneficial result. It so shocked Ludo that he decided there and then to drop everything and write a book about the case. Newspaper articles and TV programmes were all very well – Ludo himself frequently maintained that TV had little or no impact – but only a book could draw together all the threads in what had become a long and complicated saga. It wasn't just a case of wanting to expose injustice. From his writer's point of view, Ludo saw the Meehan case as a first-class story, one that gripped him. 'The thing got hold of my mind like a Chinese jigsaw puzzle,' he told a journalist. 'It became imperative to write about it.'[54] In his preface to the original edition of *A Presumption of Innocence*, subtitled *The Amazing Case of Patrick Meehan*, he wrote:

There were many things that interested me . . . about Meehan's case . . . the chance meeting the night before the verdict with his counsel. Then the dramatis personae – Meehan a criminal of unusual character and abilities; Griffiths a weird individual in a quite different way; even the surviving victim of the attack, the bingo hall owner Abraham Ross. Exceptional too were various aspects of

---

[53] *A Presumption of Innocence*.

[54] *A Presumption of Innocence*.

the case – the extraordinary 'Pat and Jim' coincidence, the police chase of Griffiths across Glasgow, the repeated confessions of Ian Waddell . . . In the end it became imperative to write about it (if for no other reason – as is said of those who want to climb Everest – than because it was there).

Having taken the decision, Ludo threw himself into his research, acting partly as writer, partly as lawyer, and partly as private detective. He set up the Paddy Meehan Defence Committee with himself as chairman and Meehan's solicitors as members. He closely inspected the scene of the crime, interviewed Abraham Ross, and retraced the journey taken by Meehan and Griffiths on the night of 5 July 1969, finding details that confirmed Meehan's description of it. He spent an enjoyable day with the BBC's David Scott, who escorted him around the Springburn district of Glasgow, where they followed the route taken by the maniacal, gun-toting Jim Griffiths prior to his death at the hands of a police marksman. But above all, he pored over the 700 pages of transcript of Meehan's trial, an analysis of which was to form the major part of his book, focusing particularly on the summing up by Lord Grant which had been so crucial to Meehan's conviction.

Grant, Ludo quickly realised, had faced a number of difficulties. His predicament was like that of the police in the case of Timothy Evans when the workmen's statements contradicted their version of events. It was that of a man who thinks he has successfully completed a jigsaw puzzle only to find that at the end of the day there are half a dozen pieces which don't seem to fit. Rather than admit that he has made mistakes and should start all over again, he hacks and hammers these missing pieces about, forcing them to fit into the finished picture. In the case of Griffiths's Lancashire accent, Grant simply brushed it aside, as if it was just one of life's little mysteries. Much more significant was the challenge of the timetable of the night of the murder. In his testimony, Meehan stated that he and Griffiths left Cairnryan (forty-five miles south of Ayr) between 1.45 and 2 p.m. and picked up the two teenage girls ten miles north of Ayr at around 3.30 p.m. On the way, he said, they stopped at Ballantrae for about ten minutes, because Griffiths wanted to inspect – with a view to stealing – a Jaguar. Even if they had gone flat out on the difficult and at times twisty road, Lord Grant's calculation left them with merely half an hour to carry out the raid before picking up the hitch-hikers at 3.30 p.m. It was absurd, Ludo concluded:

Consider what they had to do: park the car at a safe distance from the house then walk back to it; make sure
by looking through the windows that the Rosses were
asleep; go to the back of the house and cut the clothes

Timothy Evans at Paddington Station.
"The haggard, hag-ridden expression like that of a hunted animal."
© Popperfoto/Getty Images

John and Ethel Christie.
© *Topham Picturepoint*

Sir David Maxwell Fyfe.
"The nearest thing to death in life."
© *ANL/REX/Shutterstock*

John Scott Henderson QC.
His report was *"little short of a shambles."*
"One of the most extraordinary legal documents of the twentieth century."
© *TopFoto.co.uk*

INNOCENT

Patrick Meehan.
"He was not a likeable person."
© *Glasgow Herald/Evening Times*

James Griffiths.
"He liked listening to Beethoven and Tchaikovsky."
© *Daily Express*

GUILTY

Ian Waddell.
"A drunk, loose-tongued and somewhat haggard."
© *Courtesy of the Evening Times*

William 'Tank' McGuiness.
"Known to have strong psychopathic tendencies."
© *Courtesy of the Evening Times*

Lord Grant.
"Fond of a good bucket."
© Courtesy of the Scotsman

Lord Robertson.
"One of the stupidest men I have ever come across, as arrogant as he was ignorant."
© Glasgow Herald

Lord Hunter.
"Almost as big a dumbo as Lord Robertson."
© Glasgow Herald

FRAMED

(*above left*) Patrick Colin Murphy. © *Topix*

(*above right*) David Cooper. © *Daily Mail*

(*right*) Michael Graham McMahon.
© *Daily Mail*

Detective Chief Superintendent Kenneth
Drury.
*"A burly, domineering, chain-smoking
bully of a man."*
© *Associated Press*

Gareth Peirce.
"Doyenne of British criminal defence lawyers."
© REX/Shutterstock

Bryan Magee.
"An unusual figure to find on the backbenches."
© UPP/TopFoto.co.uk

Tom Sargant.
"Looked like a shabby eagle … usually covered in cigarette ash."
© PA Archive/PA Images

Lord Devlin.
"A brilliantly clever man."
© PA Archive/PA Images

Richard Hauptmann.
*"A picture that would
be seared on my mind
for ever ... the haunted
unshaven face of Richard
Hauptmann."*
© AP/Topfoto.co.uk

Ludovic Kennedy and Anna
Hauptmann.
*"Her courage and dignity, her
unwavering faith in her husband's
innocence."*

(above) Charles and Anne Morrow Lindbergh.
© Imagno/Getty Images

(right) Richard and Anna Hauptmann. *© Getty Images*

"The drama of two men – Hauptmann, a German immigrant, and Lindbergh, grandson of a Swedish immigrant, both married to devoted, God-fearing wives."

line for use later in the tie-up; go to the garage, fetch a pair of step-ladders and carry them to the side of the garage of 2 Blackburn Road; climb onto the garage roof; from there climb up the telephone pole in the corner of 4 Blackburn Place (no easy task, for the pole is two or three feet away from the garage and the first rung in it is well above the head of anyone standing on the garage roof); cut the wires, return to the ground, re-enter the Ross garage and steal a weeding tool and iron bar for breaking in; creep round to the front of the house, force open the front bedroom window very quietly so as not to disturb neighbours, and climb in; tiptoe down the corridor to the Rosses' bedroom, burst open the door and jump on them, assault them and tie them up; hit Mr Ross and go on hitting him until he has given up the keys of the safe; open the safe and take out everything in it; search the bedroom drawers and all Mr Ross's clothes; search and ransack drawers and cupboards in every other room in the house; help themselves to whisky and lemonade in the sitting room, take it to the kitchen and drink it; tie Mr Ross's feet to his hands; throw bloodstained gloves into the next-door garden; take off masks and put on shoes; leave the house and go back to the car. All this in half an hour followed by picking up a girl in a lay-by eleven or twelve minutes later! The idea was pure fantasy: but it was fantasy the jury was not invited to consider.

When it came to considering the actions of the police, Ludo was once again to be restrained by both libel law and his personal reluctance to make specific accusations of corruption. After his robust attack on Lord Grant there is a very tentative air in his approach to the police, specifically in connection with the (obviously planted) pieces of paper and the rigged identity parade. 'The police in the Glasgow area have an unenviable job,' he prefaced his remarks, 'yet there is no balking the fact that certain questions must be asked . . . Does the conduct of the police officers leave anything to be desired? Did any of these officers do anything they shouldn't have done?' Such passages inevitably conjure up thoughts of the publisher's libel lawyer breathing down Ludo's neck. Yet, once the innocence of Meehan and Griffiths was accepted, it was only logical to assume that the police must have falsified evidence. There was, for example, no way in which scraps of paper from Mr Ross's safe could have found their way into the pocket of Jim Griffiths's coat. It was, however, the identity parade that most occupied the minds of Ludo and other pro-Meehan campaigners to the exclusion of almost everything else, partly because, unlike the planting of the paper, police malpractice could be proved, thanks to several witnesses.

During the trial, when Meehan was giving evidence, several police officers stated that Abraham Ross had been the first witness to inspect the identity parade. Meehan then leaned across the dock to Joe Beltrami and hissed, 'He was the last.' Beltrami passed the message on to Fairbairn who, thinking it made little difference whether he was first or last, completely ignored it. As so often in a court case, the most significant detail was overlooked at the pertinent moment, and by the time its importance was realised it was already too late. Only long after the trial did the full implications of the order in which the witnesses inspected the identity parade slowly emerge. Desperate to find incriminating evidence to link Meehan to the murder, the police had pinned all their hopes on Mr Ross being able to identify Meehan *by his voice*, rather than by sight. They therefore devised an elaborate scheme, which turned out to be brilliantly successful. It involved three separate rooms in Glasgow Central police station. The first was a waiting room where witnesses waited to view the parade. The second contained the parade itself, consisting of Meehan and six 'stand-ins' taken off the street at random. And the third room was where witnesses, having viewed the parade, went to wait until it was all over. The worthy object was to ensure that there could be no collusion between the witnesses.

But what happened on the day? Mr Ross – who arrived from hospital accompanied by a nurse – left the waiting room first. Naturally, the other witnesses assumed that he would therefore be the first to view the parade. But he was not. Instead, he was taken straight to the final room and asked to wait. The other witnesses then all viewed the parade in turn before joining Ross in the third room. Only the two teenage hitch-hikers were able to identify Meehan. They now joined Ross, not knowing who he was, in the third room, assuming, wrongly, that he had already viewed the parade. One of them, Irene Burns, said later, 'The old man [Ross] asked me if I had picked out anyone. I told him I had, and together we discussed the parade and I described Mr Meehan to Isobel. The old man was sitting near us as we were talking.'[55]

Ross was then finally taken to the parade room. 'It must have been a dreadful moment for Mr Ross,' Ludo wrote, 'as he was helped along the corridor. He was, he thought, about to come face-to-face with the man police believed had broken into his house and murdered his wife.' When Meehan, the first man in the line-up, was asked to say, 'Shut up, shut up, we'll send an ambulance' – words that Ross remembered from the assault – the effect was dramatic. He staggered back, saying, 'That's the voice, I know it. I don't have to go any further.' He then collapsed, to the obvious alarm of police officers at the scene.

Ludo was not aware of it at the time he wrote his book, but the woman who had accompanied Ross to the waiting room was not a nurse at all. It was true that Ross had indeed been brought from hospital by

---

[55] Hunter report.

a nurse, Mrs Agnes Letham, but she had been told to wait in an office until the parade was over. (She had also been told not to come to the police station in her uniform, an order that had puzzled her at the time.) The conclusion had to be that the 'nurse' who the witnesses saw sitting with Ross in the waiting room was in fact a female police officer whose aim was to point Ross in the direction of Meehan. But despite the lengthy post-mortem carried out later by Lord Hunter, this officer was never identified and she never gave evidence at the inquiry, unlike almost everyone else involved.

Victor Gollancz published Ludo's book, *A Presumption of Innocence*, in January 1976. He had been encouraged when, prior to publication, the Secretary of State for Scotland, William Ross, had asked to see the manuscript. But four months later Ross announced 'that in consultation with the Lord Advocate he has come to the conclusion that there are no grounds that would justify the exercise of the Royal Prerogative of Mercy, or taking any other action in this case.'

All the same the book was widely reviewed, with almost every critic concluding either that Meehan was innocent or at least that there should be an official inquiry. Encouraged by this reaction, Ludo sent copies of the reviews to William Ross. All he received in reply was a brief letter of acknowledgement. There was no indication that Ross would launch an inquiry. When questioned in the House of Commons Ross stood his ground, supported by the Conservative Malcolm Rifkind, himself a Scottish lawyer and later Foreign Secretary in John Major's government, who announced that 'the alleged new evidence that is presented in Mr Kennedy's book is almost entirely obtained from those who have substantial criminal convictions'[56] – which was, as Ludo quite rightly pointed out, nonsense. The book was published but the Meehan story was far from over and eventually Ludo would have to produce a new edition of *A Presumption of Innocence* to bring it up to date.

What happened next concerned Ian Waddell's partner in crime, William 'Tank' McGuiness. McGuiness was an unstable individual who suffered from depression and made regular visits to a psychiatrist. Like Waddell he had been plagued by guilt over Meehan's wrongful imprisonment, but unlike Waddell, he knew better than to make a public confession. He did, however, confide in Joe Beltrami, who had acted as solicitor for him as he seems to have done for almost every criminal in Glasgow. Bound by a solicitor's duty of confidentiality, which is similar to that of a Catholic priest, Beltrami felt unable to report McGuiness to the police. Moreover, he was rightly wary of a man who was known to have strong psychopathic tendencies and who might be likely to react violently if he felt he had been betrayed.

---

[56] Hansard.

McGuiness must have trusted Beltrami however because he told him some important details about the murder. Most significant was the fact that when he finally left the Rosses' house to fetch his car, which was parked about half a mile away, he was stopped by two policemen to whom he gave a false name, claiming that he was on the way to the bus station. To his relief, the policemen believed him, even giving him a lift to the bus station, and McGuiness, having thanked them then doubled back to his car, fearful that he might bump into police again, especially as he had in his pocket Mr Ross's car keys and Mrs Ross's two rings. He therefore hid them under a manhole cover on the pavement. He then told Beltrami that he had never tried to retrieve them over the intervening seven years. Beltrami was excited by the idea of finding them, though what use he could have made of the discovery was never quite clear. Ludo shared his excitement and the two of them spent three hours on their hands and knees peering into a series of manholes in Ayr while Beltrami's office manager kept a lookout, but all to no avail. Throughout, Beltrami was careful not to reveal McGuiness's name to Ludo, although he had already heard it from several other sources. In the first edition of his book, he refers to him as 'McTurk'.

What dramatically and suddenly changed the situation shortly after the publication of Ludo's book was the death of McGuiness on 25 March 1976. Two weeks previously he had been found beaten and unconscious in Glasgow's Springfield Road. He died from his injuries two weeks later, so the police launched a murder inquiry. Ludo later wrote in an article in the *News of the World,* 'I believe McGuiness was killed to free Meehan. The underworld killed the real Ayr murderer.'[57] But there was never any confirmation of this theory, and Joe Beltrami dismissed it, insisting that McGuiness had been killed in a drunken brawl.

Either way, McGuiness's death released Beltrami from his oath of confidentiality and, having cleared it first with the murdered man's wife, he gave all the details of McGuiness's confession to the police. These were confirmed by Mrs McGuiness. A brief police investigation followed and details revealed by McGuiness were shown to be correct. The two officers who had given McGuiness a lift to the bus station on the night of the break-in were also identified, though neither had ever been approached to give evidence. Faced with independent confessions from Waddell and now McGuiness, the Secretary of State for Scotland, now Mr Bruce Millan, was at last forced to give way and Patrick Meehan was granted a royal pardon on 19 May 1976.

It would be nice to say that Meehan's story ended on this happy note, with his release from prison after almost seven years, a royal pardon and the promise of substantial compensation. But it did not turn out like

---

[57] *News of the World*, date unknown.

that. In the ranks of the Scottish judiciary there was a stubborn reluctance to admit that any errors had been made, let alone that the police had acted improperly. Ian Waddell himself was duly arrested and charged with the murder of Mrs Ross, but his trial turned into a retrial of Meehan, who was impeached and accused all over again of being the guilty party. Presiding over this farcical procedure was Lord Robertson, whom Ludo described as 'a large man with a pronounced Morningside accent and a florid face that he was in the habit of rubbing continually with his hand'.[58]

Ludo wrote some disparaging remarks about judges in his time, but his comments about Robertson were in a different class. 'During the next few days,' he wrote in his account of the Waddell trial, 'I watched Robertson closely and came to the conclusion he was one of the stupidest men I had ever come across, as arrogant as he was ignorant.' Robertson clung to the unusual idea that although Meehan had been pardoned by the Queen, it did not follow that he was innocent; quite the contrary. 'If you pardon someone,' he proclaimed, 'you pardon him for something he has done, and not for something he has not done.' Besides which, he added, the Secretary of State for Scotland had no right to award a pardon: 'It was an action which runs counter to the whole

---

[58] This and all other subsequent Ludo quotes relating to the Meehan case are from *Thirty-six Murders and Two Immoral Earnings* unless otherwise stated.

basis of justice and law in Scotland. Such Executive interference means that one of the greatest bulwarks in this country is threatened.' Meehan, he said, had been convicted seven years before 'on evidence which was amply justified', while 'very senior and experienced policemen' had been 'maligned, defamed and accused by Meehan of gross dereliction of duty, including perjury and the planting of evidence without, as it turns out, a shred of justification whatsoever'. As for Ludo and his ilk, 'some public support was whipped up over the years for reasons which were not entirely clear and for motives which might be imagined'.

Waddell, unsurprisingly, was acquitted, as Fairbairn explained 'because the presiding judge charged the jury saying that you could not pardon Meehan for something he had not done, so if Meehan was pardoned for doing it, Waddell couldn't have done it'. Meehan had earlier stormed out of the court, saying that his pardon was not worth the paper it was written on. Ludo admitted he had a strong urge to do the same, though not before telling Lord Robertson, 'This trial has been a farce, my Lord, and you are the chief clown.' He continued, 'Either wisely or cravenly (as I have come to believe), I refrained.'[59] Instead, he gave an interview to BBC TV in which he advised Waddell, who was currently serving a sentence for another offence, to sell the story of how he

---

[59] *Thirty-six Murders and Two Immoral Earnings.*

committed the Ayr murder to a newspaper and earn himself five thousand pounds 'or the highest offer he can get', as he could not be prosecuted for a second time.

Waddell failed to take Ludo's advice and following his release from prison went on to murder a woman called Josephine Chipperfield. In one of those biting asides that so upset members of the legal profession, Ludo commented that 'had Waddell's trial in Edinburgh not been the farce it was, and had he been sentenced to life imprisonment as he should have been, Mrs Chipperfield might have lived to a ripe old age. Did Robertson, yet another opponent of the true cause of justice, ever have the death of Mrs Chipperfield on his conscience? I rather doubt it.'[60]

The acquittal of Waddell was, in the words of Lord Hunter (later charged with chairing an official inquiry into the case) 'ill received by some lawyers, journalists and commentators. There was severe criticism of the presiding judge (Lord Robertson) as leaning too heavily in favour of the accused Waddell.'[61] There were now renewed calls for an inquiry from many of those involved,

---

[60] *Thirty-six Murders and Two Immoral Earnings.* But for his acquittal, Waddell himself could well have survived, albeit serving a life sentence for murder. As it was, like Griffiths and McGuiness, he met a violent end in 1982, murdered by one of his friends, Andy Gentle, who strangled him because he feared that Waddell would tell the police about Gentle's role in the murder of Mrs Chipperfield.

[61] This and all other subsequent quotes relating to the acquittal of Waddell come from the Hunter report unless otherwise stated.

including Ludo himself – rather surprisingly, in view of his experience of government inquiries in the case of Evans and Christie. In March 1977 the Scottish Secretary Bruce Millan, described to me by a parliamentary colleague as 'colourless but meticulous', who had been savagely attacked by Lord Robertson for daring to interfere in the proceedings of the Scottish courts, finally agreed to hold an inquiry, though not in public. The man chosen for the job was yet another Scottish judge, Lord (Jack) Hunter, a popular figure with his fellow lawyers, whose appointment was generally welcomed.

The Patrick Meehan Defence Committee met to decide whether or not to cooperate with Lord Hunter. The difficulty was that, having continually demanded an inquiry, their position would be compromised if they now rejected the whole idea. All the same, there were misgivings. At first sight, Ludo recorded in a postscript to the second edition of his book, 'the depressingly restrictive terms of reference' – the inquiry would be in private with no powers of subpoena – 'seemed to us to be establishing a good basis for a whitewash'. On the other hand, Hunter 'was represented to us as a man of great intellectual integrity and independence of mind who would in no way be influenced by the views of anyone, including his colleagues on the Scottish bench'. Much the same view of Hunter came from committee member Beltrami, who records, en passant, that Ludo would still have preferred an English lawyer, such as

Louis Blom-Cooper – not surprising as Blom-Cooper had written a glowing review of Ludo's book. In the end the committee decided to assist Hunter and persuaded Meehan to do the same, even though he had little confidence in the judge – not to be wondered at in view of all that had happened to date.

Meehan's misgivings turned out to be more than justified, and even Beltrami was forced to revise his opinion after long sessions – one lasting five hours – with Lord Hunter. The judge had done a great deal of research, Beltrami noted, and his questions were very searching, but he was plainly not prepared to share Beltrami's long-held conviction that Meehan was innocent.

Hunter's report took five years to complete and was finally published in August 1982. It was 400,000 words long, weighed five and a half pounds and had cost £330,826 to produce. The judge stated that he had interviewed no fewer than 300 witnesses, including Lord Mountbatten and Enoch Powell. Most of these people were impressed by Hunter's apparent grasp of the essentials. He seemed to be asking all the right questions. But many a litigant has had his hopes raised by the way a judge conducts a case only to have those hopes dashed when he reaches his final judgement. This was exactly what happened with Hunter. He was critical of many of the police officers and lawyers involved in the case, often with justification, but on the central issues of the case, he showed no sign of the independence of mind with which he had been credited. He was particularly scathing about Meehan himself, plainly unimpressed by the fact that he had spent seven years in prison for a crime he didn't commit and for which he had since received a royal pardon. Hunter called him a 'glib inventive liar, one of those people who appear unable or unwilling to tell the truth even when to do so might be to their own advantage'.[62]

Hunter would have been horrified to have that judgement thrown back at him, such is the self-righteousness common to so many judges. Yet when it came to some of his own findings, he too could just as well have been accused of an inability – or an unwillingness – to tell the truth. The best example was his treatment of the identity parade at which Mr Ross claimed to have identified Meehan as one of his two assailants from the sound of his voice. Meehan and his supporters, notably his son, had done an exhaustive job gathering evidence from all those they had been able to trace who had witnessed the parade, including four of the six stand-ins, all of whom told Hunter that Abraham Ross was the last person to view the line-up. The two solicitors who had been present said the same.

Hunter was well aware of the difficulty he faced. If what all six men remembered was true, it followed that the policemen had perjured themselves at Meehan's

---

[62] Hunter report.

trial, thereby appearing to confirm the allegation that
the identity parade had been deliberately rigged. This
was a step too far for Hunter who now found that,
for a variety of specious reasons, the witnesses were
not reliable. A particular problem was posed by the
presence at the parade of Mr Peter McCann, one of
two solicitors representing Meehan. For McCann was
no mere solicitor but a city councillor and, at the time,
Lord Provost of Glasgow. His evidence to Hunter was
emphatic: 'So in came Ross – last, last, last, last. In he
came.' Hunter's response was truly bizarre:

> It appears probable that McCann subsequently convinced
> himself that Ross was last, a conclusion which may have
> been supported in his mind by a recollection of the inter-
> ruption in the proceedings at the identification parade
> after Ross had collapsed. The potency of suggestion and
> the dangers of reconstruction in such circumstances have
> already been mentioned. Lawyers may sometimes be just
> as susceptible to such influences as other people, particu-
> larly if they allow their emotions or personal beliefs to
> become involved in a case.[63]

'It appears probable' is a phrase that resounds
throughout the 1300 pages of the Hunter report, often
with the variation 'it is not improbable', suggesting

---

[63] Hunter report.

that the 'dangers of reconstruction' were not confined to the witnesses.

But it was when he came to his final conclusion that Hunter passed from improbability to absurdity. For whatever reason, in his preliminary remarks he had quoted some words of Sir Daniel Brabin ('stale evidence is bad evidence') and it was Brabin who, coincidentally, had conducted the Rillington Place inquiry in 1966 and had reached the ludicrous conclusion, savagely attacked by Ludo, that although Christie had murdered Evans's baby Geraldine (the crime for which Evans had been hanged), Evans had probably murdered his wife – a theory for which there was no evidence whatsoever but one which conveniently absolved the lawyers and the police from any blame for the execution of an innocent man. Now Lord Hunter was to reach an equally ridiculous conclusion with the same aim in mind. Rather than acquit Meehan and Griffiths (thereby casting doubt on the precious integrity of the police) and convict McGuiness and Waddell, he proposed at the end of his five-year investigation that *all four* men were involved in the Ayr murder. It was possible, he admitted, for the crime to be carried out by two men but this was apparently 'against the probabilities' and 'improbable in the highest degree'. So Waddell and McGuiness had carried out the break-in while Meehan and Griffiths were standing by in case their services were needed. 'It cannot be disproved,' Hunter wrote, in another variation on the improbability theme, 'that Meehan and Griffiths were not a follow-up team with the role of dealing with the safe or safes that were believed to be in the bungalow.' (He managed to overlook the fact that McGuiness specialised in safe-blowing and would have required no assistance from the other two.) But safe-blowing was not the only issue. 'The assailants would probably' – that word again – 'need a look-out as the possibility of shouts and screaming could not be discounted.' All in all, it 'cannot be concluded with any degree of confidence that Meehan and Griffiths did not play some part in the crime'. Hunter ploughed on, no doubt hoping that his pompous turn of phrase, his frequent use of the double negative and the occasional Latin word would, if repeated often enough, persuade the reader of the validity of his case: 'Nor in particular is the available information considered to justify that they were neither at the locus nor handled any of the proceeds of the crime.'

Though many years later Ludo was to damn Lord Hunter as having shown himself to be 'almost as big a dumbo as Lord Robertson'[64], at the time he was slightly less provocative: 'Lord Hunter is so agreeable a person, was so courteous and patient with his witnesses, has been so painstaking in the assembly of the mass of material presented to him that one hesitates to strike

---

[64] *Thirty-six Murders and Two Immoral Earnings.*

a discordant note. All the same it must be done. His report is a nonsense.'[65]

If lawyers took comfort from Hunter's nonsensical conclusions, the report did little to rehabilitate Paddy Meehan, a man who had been granted a free pardon only to be told subsequently by a High Court judge that he had been guilty all along – a view that was now confirmed by another judge following a five-year investigation. Meehan could take some comfort only from a belated award of £50,000 compensation (he had previously rejected a derisory offer of £7,500). In the years that followed he continued the campaign for his restitution. He had already published a book, *Innocent Villain* (1978), which preceded the Hunter report, and he later wrote another, *Framed by MI5* (1989), in which he claimed that he was victim of a conspiracy by the security services in revenge for the assistance he had given to the spy George Blake in his escape from Wandsworth Prison, where they had both been prisoners. Belligerent to the end, Meehan never resumed his criminal activities and took instead to selling double-glazing and, appropriately, burglar alarms. He later moved from Glasgow to Port Talbot in Wales, where he died from throat cancer in 1994.

As for Ludo, the case had a preposterous postscript. He and Moira had moved to a house in Edinburgh two

---

[65] *Thirty-six Murders and Two Immoral Earnings.*

years after the Meehan case was concluded and he reap-
plied to join the prestigious Muirhead golf club on the
East Lothian coast where he had often played as a guest
of other members. The snag was that the club was patronised by a good many Scottish lawyers, a number
of whom were friends of another prominent member,
Lord Robertson, the judge who had refused to recognise Meehan's royal pardon. As a result, Ludo was
blackballed. It was an unsurprising reaction from men
who saw Ludo as a class traitor. The duty of the son
of a Scottish naval officer and a product of Eton and
Oxford was to stand by judges, not throw mud at them.
Ludo, who prided himself on his ability to play the occasional round with judges whom he attacked (including
the Lord Chief Justice, Lord Lane), surely welcomed the
support he received on this occasion from another mav-
erick Scottish golfer – the editor of the *Sunday Express*,
John Junor. In his column, Junor questioned the two
unidentified members who had sponsored Ludo: 'Are
these two men now going to resign from the club which
has spat not just in their nominee's face but also in their
own? I hope so. Besides, who would want to remain a
member of the club which, by rejecting an interesting
chap like Mr Kennedy, reveals itself as a bunch of dull,
sanctimonious, po-faced Scottish legal creeps?'[66]

---

[66] John Junor, *The Best of JJ*, Sidgwick and Jackson Ltd., 1981.

Chapter 3

The Luton Post Office Murder

Some time in May 1971, a cockney criminal, Stephen Murphy – like many crooks an energetic and resourceful man – called at the *Private Eye* offices at 34 Greek Street in London's Soho. Murphy had previously visited a number of newspapers hoping to interest them in the story of his son Patrick who, he claimed, had been wrongly sentenced, along with two others, to life imprisonment for a murder he had nothing whatsoever to do with. The press had shown little interest and, as it had been for many in the past and as it would be in the future, *Private Eye* was his last port of call.

Perhaps Murphy was hoping to interest the *Eye*'s chief reporter, Paul Foot, who for some time had been campaigning in the magazine on behalf of James Hanratty, hanged in 1962 for the so-called A6 murder. But Paul was not in the office that day. Instead Murphy was directed to Patrick Marnham. He had joined *Private Eye* in 1966 after answering an advertisement for an 'editorial assistant, preferably graduate with knowledge of politics and journalism'. As editor at the time, I was impressed by the young Marnham and gave him the job, whereupon he abandoned his previous ambition of becoming a barrister and took to a life of journalism, to which he was very well suited. He worked for the *Eye* full-time for two years before moving to Fleet Street, but returned as a regular contributor in 1970. He launched the magazine's notorious 'Grovel' gossip column and in 1976 stood beside me in the dock of the Old Bailey's Number One Court accused of criminal libel by the sinister financier Sir James Goldsmith.

Marnham took a shine to Stephen Murphy and was impressed by his conviction of his son's innocence, his determination to fight for his release by every possible means, and his lack of any embarrassment about his own criminal milieu and that of his son. Both of them had records, as did two other East Enders who had been convicted of the murder alongside Patrick – David Cooper and Michael McMahon. Posing as Patrick's barrister, Marnham visited him in Pentonville with Murphy senior, whom he also accompanied on a search for potential witnesses who might support Murphy's alibi. (At one stage the father's enthusiasm had to be curbed by a lecture from Paul Foot, who warned him that any witness must be bona fide and not just 'a friend of the family'.) In the meantime, Marnham recommended a solicitor, Wendy Mantle, who worked with *Private Eye*'s libel lawyer Geoffrey Bindman. Stephen Murphy showed his gratitude by offering Marnham a succession of rewards – an antique table, a well-paid but bogus job bundling copies of the *Sunday Express* ('You've only got to go once') and a half share in a London taxi. Murphy found it hard to understand why the young journalist continued to turn down all these tempting gifts.

The story Stephen Murphy told Marnham, which was published in *Private Eye* in May 1971 under the heading 'Mathews Gospel', was the first inkling the public gained of what was to be one of the most shameful episodes in British legal history (it was to be some time before the full extraordinary story would be told by Ludo in his book *Wicked Beyond Belief*). The article began: 'On 10th September 1969 at about 6.05 p.m. Reginald Stevens, the manager of the High Town Post Office in Luton, was shot dead in the nearby car park of Barclays Bank as he was about to drive home.'

The weapon (a sawn-off shotgun) had been fired into his chest at close range and forensic evidence later suggested that it had gone off accidentally during a struggle. It was thought that the object of the attack was to obtain the postmaster's keys prior to breaking the safe. The four men involved in the crime had then driven off in a van at great speed. One of them, Alfred Mathews, was later identified by an alert witness, who noted the number of his car when he picked it up at Luton Station, where he had parked it prior to the raid.

Arrested by the policeman in charge of investigating the crime, Commander Ken Drury of the Flying Squad, Mathews made a highly fanciful statement that he later repeated in court. He claimed he had been inveigled into travelling to Luton with three other men to pick up some parcels in exchange for a payment of ten pounds. On arrival in the town at about 6 p.m., he said, the three others left him at the station and drove off in a van, only to return shortly afterwards in a state of panic. One of them shouted, 'Get going, you have shot him.' The driver of the van, Mathews stated on oath, was Patrick Murphy.

Astonishingly, considering the improbable nature of this account, Mathews had been allowed by the Director of Public Prosecutions (in the person of one J. E. Leck) to turn Queen's evidence. In other words, he was granted immunity in exchange for providing vital information about his accomplices. (This was only the first in a long series of scandalous developments in the story.) Yet Commander Drury was well aware that two witnesses had already failed to identify Murphy as the driver of the van. Both of these witnesses had been near the crime scene and both had seen the van drive off at conspicuously high speed. Moreover, both had seen the driver clearly, describing him as hollow-cheeked, mid-forties and wearing a hat. Murphy was a slim, red-haired twenty-six-year-old. In 'Mathews Gospel', Marnham described the fifty-three-year-old Mathews as 'medium built, with distinctive grey hair, hollow-cheeked and sharp features'. (A picture of him with swept-back hair bears a marked resemblance to Samuel Beckett.)

Both witnesses gave statements to the police but both were advised not to assist Murphy's lawyers, who were naturally anxious to secure their help. They did, however, come forward when the three convicted men made an application to present their cases to the Court of Appeal, during which lawyers argued that if Mathews drove the van and subsequently named Murphy as the driver, his evidence, on which all three were convicted, was deeply suspect. Rejecting the application, the judges – Lord Justice Fenton Atkinson, Mr Justice Lyell and Mr Justice Mars-Jones – said of Mathews, 'Whether he was the actual driver of the van, or exactly what part he was playing, perhaps does not matter.' (The inclusion of the word 'perhaps' in this verdict, which suggests perhaps it might matter a great deal, is a fine example of judicial humbug.)

By this stage, it was apparent to a growing number of people, if not to the judges of the Court of Appeal, that there was something very fishy about the case of the Luton Post Office murder. It was not just Mathews's identification of Murphy and the two others; the whole account of his involvement was ludicrous. Why would a life-long criminal go all the way to Luton just to pick up some parcels in exchange for ten pounds? So why had he been allowed to turn Queen's evidence? And what was the role of the police officer in charge of the investigation, Commander Ken Drury, by now Head of the Flying Squad at Scotland Yard?

Marnham's article led quickly to a *Private Eye* follow-up. Two issues later, in June 1971, he reported that, as a result of his previous piece, two men, Fred Stephens and Terry Leonard, had made statements about Mathews. They claimed that Mathews had tried to enlist them for a raid on the Luton post office four years earlier, telling them that the safe contained £12,000. They visited the post office with Mathews but opted out when he told them he intended to use a gun.

The two *Eye* articles aroused the interest of freelance reporter Bill Thomson, who was then working at the *Ilford Recorder*. He managed to secure an interview with Mathews, who, like many criminals – Ian Waddell was another – was unable to resist the lure of publicity and the possibility of making some big money at the same time. (It is also probable that, like Waddell – and even John Christie – Mathews experienced feelings of guilt about his role in the conviction of an innocent man.) Thomson gained access to Mathews with the help of Mathews's brother Albert and they met at Albert's house in Caernarvon Avenue, Ilford. 'When I arrived,' Thomson recorded, 'Mathews was already there. He was sitting in a straight-back chair in front of the window, leaning on a dining table. He maintained this position throughout the interview which lasted one hour and twenty minutes.'[67]

Mathews, who struck Thomson as being highly nervous, chain-smoked throughout the eighty minutes. He talked incoherently and when agitated would fall back on religion, claiming, 'I'm a God-fearing man ... God guided me through all this.' Finding this hard to stomach, Thomson countered, 'I'm sure Our Lord would not approve of an innocent man being sent to prison for twenty years.' At this, Mathews became 'agitated and aggressive'. Only twice in the course of the interview, during which he was mostly unintelligible or accusatory, did he drop his guard. Of the murder of Reginald Stevens, the Luton postmaster, he muttered, 'I didn't know the old fella was going to die.' Later, Thomson asked Mathews if Murphy had been involved in the shooting. 'Without looking at me and obviously without thinking he said, "I might have made ..." He never completed the sentence but I was of the opinion that he was going to say "mistake". Mathews then accused me of trying to trap him. He became angry and I decided to leave.'

Encouraged by Marnham's and Thomson's interest, Stephen Murphy continued to fight for his son's release and was lucky to secure an ally in the shape of Tom Sargant, brother of Sir William Sargant, the psychiatrist

---

[67] Ludo's book, *Wicked Beyond Belief*.

and author of *Battle for the Mind* (see page 41). Tom Sargant was a highly principled campaigner and a parliamentary candidate for Sir Richard Acland's Christian socialist party Common Wealth. He later joined Justice, an organisation of lawyers devoted to the protection of human rights, and became its leading light despite a lack of legal training. 'Sargant,' says his entry in the *Dictionary of National Biography*, 'looked like a shabby eagle. Tall, angular and untidy, he was usually covered in cigarette ash.'

Eventually there were a number of hopeful developments, one of which was quite unexpected. For some time, a number of journalists on the *Sunday People*, encouraged by the proprietor Hugh Cudlipp, had been conducting a large-scale investigation into the pornography barons in London's Soho, particular interest being shown in allegations about corrupt police involvement in the trade. It was common knowledge on Fleet Street that the police were operating what amounted to a protection racket, guaranteeing a number of traders freedom from prosecution in exchange for regular payments, gifts and assorted perks and favours. One of the richest, most successful operators was James Humphreys, a one-time inmate of Dartmoor who, with the help of his redheaded wife Rusty, a former stripper, had built up a highly profitable empire of strip clubs and 'dirty book shops'. On the proceeds, he had bought himself a Rolls-Royce and a country mansion in Sussex while maintaining excellent relations with a number of senior policemen.

On 27 February 1972 the *Sunday People* published an astonishing scoop. It revealed that Humphreys, the so-called 'emperor of porn', and Rusty had recently returned from a two-week holiday in Cyprus with none other than Commander Ken Drury, who by now was head of Scotland Yard's supposedly elite Flying Squad, and his wife Joan. And it appeared that this was not an isolated incident. Humphreys and Drury, as Barry Cox, John Shirley and Martin Short would later reveal in *The Fall of Scotland Yard* (1977), had known each other for some time. They had been to the FA Cup Final together, and one of Drury's sons, a motor mechanic, had serviced Humphreys's Rolls-Royce. While in Cyprus, Drury and Humphreys had even discussed going into business together as hotel proprietors. Humphreys would later reveal that he paid Drury one hundred pounds a week to prevent any police interference in his activities.

The most astonishing thing about Drury's behaviour was his recklessness. Though he must have been aware of growing press interest in the flourishing porn industry, he made no attempt to practise discretion, to the extent of registering in the Cypriot hotel with his police rank and giving his address as 'New Scotland Yard'. Invited by the *News of the World* to offer an explanation for the trip, he claimed that he had gone to Cyprus to search for Ronald Biggs, who was wanted for his part in the Great Train Robbery of 1963. This was almost as unconvincing as Mathews's claim that he had gone to Luton to pick up some parcels in exchange for ten pounds.

For Murphy, Cooper and McMahon, the exposure of Drury seemed like a windfall. At their trial, the commander had given evidence as a senior, highly respected police officer with thirty-six years' service whom the Home Office had recently shortlisted for the post of national coordinator of the country's nine regional crime squads. Now, his downfall was swift and sudden. He was immediately suspended following the story in the *People*, and two months later ceased to be a police officer.

Surely the fact that the policeman who was largely responsible for Murphy, Cooper and McMahon's conviction had been shown to be corrupt and was likely to face prosecution would influence the judges in the Court of Appeal? It was not to be, thereby showing once again that what the layman thinks is important, obvious and a matter of simple common sense may well be dismissed as irrelevant in the eyes of the law.

More hopeful, from Patrick Murphy's point of view, was the recent discovery of a new witness – Terence Edwards – who was able to confirm his alibi for the day of the Luton murder. On the strength of Edwards's evidence the Home Secretary Robert Carr now referred Murphy's case back to the Court of Appeal. It took almost a year to come to court while lawyers tried unsuccessfully to bring additional evidence in Murphy's favour, but, when the case was finally heard in November 1973, Lord Widgery the Lord Chief Justice was so impressed by Edwards's testimony – 'a man of good character – his answers seemed to be convincing – his demeanour was impressive'[68] – that he allowed the appeal and ordered Murphy's conviction to be quashed.

Although the Court of Appeal expressly refrained from offering a view about the convictions of Cooper and McMahon, they drew encouragement from the verdict, for if Mathews was shown to be wrong about Murphy, how could he be relied on when he identified the other two men? They and their lawyers therefore felt confident as they prepared for yet another appeal.

The prospects were favourable. The Labour Party was re-elected in 1974 under Harold Wilson, who appointed the distinctly liberal figure of Roy Jenkins as Home Secretary. More important from David Cooper's point of view was the election of Bryan Magee as his local MP for Leyton, a seat he inherited from the retiring member, Patrick Gordon Walker. Magee was an unusual figure to find on the backbenches. An intellectual from a working-class family in East London, he had studied philosophy at Oxford, later becoming a visiting fellow at All Souls and occupying a number of academic posts

---

[68] *Wicked Beyond Belief.*

in the United States as well as in the UK. An authority on music, particularly opera, Magee had, like Ludo, pursued a very successful career as a broadcaster, interviewing philosophers on the BBC and judges on ITV. But his career was now to take an unexpected turn as he became involved in a long-running murder mystery and a campaign for justice. He inherited Cooper's cause from his predecessor Gordon Walker, who was too big a fish in the Labour hierarchy to find the time to deal with a complex legal brief. Magee, however, took his duties towards his constituents very seriously. He studied the Luton papers carefully and visited Cooper in prison, quickly becoming convinced that, even if guilty, he should never have been convicted on the flimsy evidence produced at his trial, least of all the allegations made by Mathews. The possibility of an innocent man being kept in prison for years filled him with indignation, though he was not prepared to include McMahon in his campaign. McMahon was not his constituent, and in any case, in common with several others, Magee felt that the evidence against McMahon was stronger. Not only had a witness, Mrs Crawley, picked out McMahon from a photograph (see below), but two men, Weyers and Jackson, fellow inmates at Leicester Prison had testified at the trial that McMahon had confessed to the Luton killing. (The fact that both of these prisoners subsequently received a share of the reward money from Drury's handout and both had their sentences cut to thank them for their cooperation ought to have aroused suspicions.)

Magee's indignation was shared by Cooper's new solicitor, Gareth Peirce. (Wendy Mantle, Patrick Murphy's lawyer, was now also representing McMahon.) Gareth was a young woman fresh out of law school and now working for Ben Birnberg, a left-winger well known for his work on behalf of the victims of injustice. If Cooper had any doubts about her lack of experience, they would have been quickly dispelled by her powers of application and her quiet determination to root out the truth. But, like Magee, Gareth was not going to jump to any quick conclusions. On her first visit to Cooper in Wormwood Scrubs he asked her if she believed he was innocent of the Luton murder. She answered truthfully and with typical caution that, having read all the papers, it was clear to her that the evidence against him was very flimsy and that she *thought* he was innocent.

The more she pursued her enquiries, however, the more that initial feeling hardened into a certainty. One of her first self-appointed tasks was to write to the Post Office, which on the orders of the Postmaster General John Stonehouse had offered a £5,000 reward for information the day after the shooting. Who, Gareth wondered, had benefited? Rather to her surprise, the Post Office sent her a list of the ten beneficiaries, headed by Alfred Mathews, who had apparently received £2,000 (equal to about £20,000 today). A letter from a Post

Office official to Ken Drury, thanking him for handling the payment and congratulating him 'on the successful outcome of the murder inquiry', came to light later.

The reward money was one thing. But Gareth also discovered the existence of over eight hundred statements taken by the police within days of the murder, not one of which was disclosed to the defence. Typical of these was a succession of statements made by Mrs Crawley, who had been chatting to her neighbour at the back of some houses facing the car park where the murder took place. Interviewed on the evening of the crime, she first said that she had seen a man running from the postmaster's car to a van that was already moving. 'I wouldn't recognise him again,' she admitted. But in her later statements Mrs Crawley's story changed dramatically. Now she said she had seen not one but three men. Not only that, but having said she would not be able to recognise even one man, she now gave detailed descriptions of all three, including height, hairstyles and clothing. Finally, at the trial, she testified that she had identified McMahon when Drury had shown her a picture of him. Mrs Crawley, like several other helpful witnesses, received £200 in Drury's share-out of the reward money. The crucial witness, McNair, who had identified Mathews and taken down his car registration, did not receive a penny.

Gareth Peirce went on to track down a number of new witnesses, of whom the most important, from Cooper's point of view, was Morris Lerman, a Jewish tailor with a shop in Mare Street, Hackney. When first arrested, Cooper had told Drury that he had been in Lerman's shop to collect a suit at about 5 p.m. on 10 September 1969, about an hour before the shooting. Realising that any confirmation of this story would destroy the prosecution's case against Cooper, Drury sent two of his officers to Mare Street to interview Lerman. The tailor was insistent. He remembered Cooper visiting the shop at precisely the time he'd told the police and saying that he had to be in court the next day to answer charges about a stolen washing machine. The following day, Drury sent his two officers back to the shop to try to persuade Lerman to change his story. 'They tried to turn me against him. They asked how I would like it if one of my relatives had been shot in the guts,' Lerman recalled in an affidavit for Gareth Peirce. But he refused to retract his earlier statement. Ludo does not say so, but he must have been reminded of the workmen at 10 Rillington Place whose timetable failed to coincide with the police's version of events and who had to be coerced into altering their story.

His underlings having failed to make Lerman change his evidence, Drury drove to the tailor's shop himself and, in accordance with his policy of always interviewing on home ground, made Lerman sit in his car, telling him that he was not a man who made mistakes or put his finger on the wrong man. Drury was a large, powerfully built man with a bullying manner, but Lerman was adamant, adding that he knew his date was right as he remembered there was a Jewish holiday that weekend, which had prevented him from finishing Cooper's suit on time. Drury was not prepared to give up, though. He named Lerman as a prosecution witness, which prevented the defence team from calling him or even interviewing him prior to the trial. 'The making of Lerman into a prosecution witness,' Gareth Peirce wrote subsequently, 'had devastating consequences for Cooper.'[69]

Drury's handling of Lerman quite clearly contravened the Criminal Justice Act of 1967, which stipulated that the police were not permitted to interview alibi witnesses without the consent of the defence solicitors. But the Commander, who was well known for his cavalier habit of ignoring regulations, was now the subject of more serious allegations in the press – namely, that he had conspired with Mathews to convict three men whom he knew to be innocent, and that he had shared Mathews's £2,000 reward from the Post Office. A year or so after his first interview with Mathews, Bill Thomson re-established contact with him using the possibility of selling his story to one of the Sunday newspapers as a carrot. Thomson had been told by informers in the criminal fraternity that Drury had received some

---

[69] CCRC submission, G. Peirce.

of the reward, while Mathews's brother had already told him that Mathews had been given only half of the promised £2,000. Pressed by Thomson over the course of a two-hour interview, Mathews, without ever being specific, made it clear that he had shared his reward money with Drury.

If that were true then, along with other evidence of suborned witnesses and concealed evidence, it pointed to a conspiracy of truly shocking proportions. But, as in the Meehan case, the defence lawyers were well aware that judges were always reluctant to recognise corrupt practice by police officers. Proof of this was provided by Sir Frederick Lawton, who sat in a subsequent appeal by Cooper and McMahon and later told the Royal Commission on Criminal Procedure that, in fifteen years of sitting as a judge in the Court of Appeal, where he heard as many as eight hundred appeals each year, he could not recollect a single assertion of police malpractice.[70] This was a truly astonishing claim which, if true, is proof of the reluctance of barristers to make charges of corruption against the police – even at a time, the 1970s, when corruption in the police force was so widespread that, in 1972, a new commissioner, Robert Mark, was appointed by the government with the specific aim of stamping it out and charging the worst offenders.

---

[70] Royal Commission on Criminal Procedure, 1981.

Drury aside, the strength of Cooper and McMahon's appeal lay in the discrediting of Mathews's evidence. Now that the Court of Appeal had accepted that his identification of Patrick Murphy as the driver of the van was unsound, how could there be any confidence in his identification of Cooper and McMahon? It was not as if he had claimed to have caught merely a glimpse of Murphy. As Gareth Peirce wrote in her brief to counsel in a subsequent appeal, Mathews's evidence at the original trial had described 'a detailed sighting of Murphy over a sustained period of time in which he could describe in precise detail his glasses, his coat (both colour and length, even though Murphy was sitting down at the time), and graphic descriptions of him shouting and vaulting into the car'.

The latest appeal hearing opened on 10 February 1975 before Lord James, Lord Ashworth and the Lord Chief Justice, Lord Widgery, a ruddy-faced former wartime colonel.[71] The appeal began badly for Cooper and McMahon when they were brought into court handcuffed to each other. When Cooper's barrister Bryan Anns asked for the handcuffs to be removed as, apart from the discomfort, it made it virtually impossible

---

[71] A few years earlier, in 1971, Widgery had been appointed by Prime Minister Edward Heath to investigate the notorious 'Bloody Sunday' shootings by British troops of innocent civilian demonstrators in Londonderry. (Reminded earlier by Heath of the great influence of propaganda, Widgery duly exonerated the Army in his report published in April 1972.)

for his client to take notes, Widgery refused. Worse was to come. Bryan Anns had earlier asked the court for leave to cross-examine Mathews about his evidence at the original trial. Mathews had been subpoenaed and was waiting outside the courtroom to be summoned. But Widgery ruled that it was most unusual to cross-examine witnesses in appeals hearings and refused to admit him. ('I could not believe my ears,'[72] Bryan Magee wrote later.) When it came to the involvement of Drury, Anns read a statement from Bill Thomson in which the journalist described his most recent interview with Mathews, during which it had emerged that Drury had taken a share of the reward money. But Widgery didn't want to know. 'We're not investigating Drury's credibility, are we?' he asked testily.

Throughout the hearing, Widgery seemed determined to dismiss the many discrepancies that were put forward by the defence. Anns argued, for example, that Mrs Crawley was an unreliable witness as she had originally stated that she had seen only one unrecognisable man, before positively identifying McMahon as one of three men she had observed in the car park. Widgery replied, 'Perhaps she was only being modest when she first stated she wouldn't be able to identify him' – an extraordinary remark that could only be interpreted as an obscure kind of judicial joke, or possibly a sign of

[72] Ludo's book, *Wicked Beyond Belief*.

the early stages of dementia which in the end forced him to retire. Gareth Peirce remembers Bryan Anns saying to her during the hearing, 'The Lord Chief's not himself.'

But then, as so often happens in court, Widgery said something which suggested that he had finally seen the light. When the prosecuting counsel, Victor Durand, raised the question of whether Mathews had lied when identifying Murphy as the driver of the van, Widgery interposed, 'If Mathews was lying about Murphy, doesn't the prosecution against Mr Cooper and Mr McMahon collapse like a pack of cards?' – the very point which their lawyers were arguing. McMahon turned excitedly to Cooper and whispered, 'I think we've won it.'[73]

But it was not to be. The pack of cards stayed miraculously intact. After a brief fifteen-minute conference, the three judges returned to announce that the appeal was dismissed. Later, in a written judgement, they persisted with the view that in identifying Murphy as the driver of the van Mathews could have been mistaken – this despite the fact that two witnesses had identified Mathews himself as the van's driver – and the fact that he had falsely identified Murphy did not necessarily mean that he had been equally wrong about Cooper and McMahon. The verdict was greeted with dismay and incredulity by all of those who had followed the

---

[73] *Wicked Beyond Belief.*

case. Gareth Peirce referred to the 'breathtaking absurdity' of the judgement, while Bryan Magee wrote, 'Even as a politician I have rarely heard such a bad argument put forward seriously in public by people who are supposed to be intelligent . . . [T]heir combination of complacency, brutal indifference and lack of common sense was one I was unprepared to encounter in High Court judges.' But were the judges simply stupid and pig-headed? Justice campaigner Tom Sargant thought differently: 'The heart of the matter,' he told the *Guardian* (date unknown), 'was that they didn't want to open the floodgates. They didn't want everything to come out.'

Such a view is by no means as wild as some readers may think. Only a few years later, in 1980, Lord Denning – Master of the Rolls and a widely admired judge – made a memorable and much-quoted statement when upholding an appeal by the West Midlands Police, whom the Birmingham Six had accused of assault and perjury:

> If the six men win, it will mean that the police were guilty of perjury, that they were guilty of violence and threats, that the confessions were involuntary and were improperly admitted in evidence and that the convictions were erroneous. This would mean that the Home Secretary would either have to recommend they be pardoned or he would have to remit the case to the Court of Appeal. This

is such an appalling vista that every sensible person in the land would say 'It cannot be right that these actions go any further.'[74]

Denning was reviled for speaking in this way but he was perhaps doing no more than articulating opinions which – while probably not, as he foolishly thought, held by 'every sensible person in the land' – were nevertheless held by a great many judges. It was preferable to imprison half a dozen possibly innocent men than jeopardise the prestige of the police and courts by exposing a litany of corruption, perjury and even torture. In the Luton case, Lord Widgery and his colleagues may well have resented having been told what to do by the Home Secretary – to cross-examine Mathews in particular – but they must also have thought of the consequences if they upheld the appeal. Such a judgement would mean acknowledging that three men had been wrongly sentenced to life imprisonment as a result of a conspiracy orchestrated by a corrupt policeman and a hardened criminal; that evidence had been fabricated and suppressed; and that Drury and Mathews had shared between them a large sum of money provided by the

---

[74] A very similar argument was advanced by the Scottish judge Lord Hunter in his report on the Patrick Meehan case when confronted by irrefutable evidence that the police had rigged an identity parade and later committed perjury. If that were so, he said, it would do immense damage and long-lasting harm to the proper administration of criminal justice.

State as a reward. Here was another 'appalling vista' that simply could not be contemplated, even if it meant that two innocent men – albeit two known criminals, the judges may have reassured themselves – should remain in prison for the duration. They did not appear to worry too much about the possible eventual exposure of a cover-up that would compound the damage done to the reputation of the courts.

Following the failure of the appeal, Tom Sargant and Bryan Magee both appeared on an hour-long BBC *Panorama* programme. But Magee, who had also written an article for *The Times* on the extraordinary verdict, was already coming to the conclusion that a media campaign would have little effect or might even prove counter-productive. Senior judges famously resented press interference, and several had expressed dismay that the insurance fraudster Emil Savundra had been subjected to 'trial by television' during his sensational interview with David Frost in 1967. Aside from his political contacts, Magee had a powerful friend and ally in the shape of the retired judge Lord Devlin, whom he had met some years previously when conducting a series of interviews with judges for ITV. Born into a Catholic family in 1905, Devlin had joined the Dominican Order as a novice in his teens but later embarked on a career at the Bar, eventually becoming a highly respected judge in the Court of Appeal and the author of several books on the law and especially its relation to morality. One of his books, *Easing the Passing*, was an account of the famous trial, over which he presided, of an Eastbourne GP, John Bodkin Adams, accused but acquitted of murdering one of his patients, a rich old lady, in order to profit from her will. A brilliantly clever man, he told Magee that he had once been in the middle of a summing up when he realised he had reached the wrong decision, but he was able to change tack and come to a directly opposite conclusion to his original one without anyone noticing.

Advised by Devlin, who had no wish at this stage to make his views public, Magee set about lobbying the Home Office minister Alex Lyon. Magee was assisted by Gareth Peirce, who provided him with a comprehensive rundown of all the evidence that pointed to a miscarriage of justice, including the testimony of a new witness, a Mr Slade, who claimed to have seen Cooper twice in London on the afternoon of the murder. Realising that the case was not going to go away, in April 1976 Home Secretary Roy Jenkins finally decided to refer it once more to the Court of Appeal, the first time that a referral had been made twice. On this occasion, Jenkins insisted that the judges must allow cross-examination of witnesses.

The case opened on 12 July 1976 before Lord Justice Roskill, Lord Justice Lawton and Mr Justice Wien.[75] This

---

[75] Coincidentally, three months earlier, it was Wien who gave James Goldsmith leave to prosecute me and Patrick Marnham for criminal libel.

time the judges gave way to the Home Secretary and agreed to allow cross-examination of witnesses with the result that on day two of the hearing Alfred Mathews and Ken Drury were finally called to give evidence. Bryan Magee, who sat in the courtroom throughout all six days of the hearing, wrote later:

> The courtroom was so small that I was no more than a few paces from everyone else in it, including the judges. I retain from the proceedings some of the most vivid impressions of my life. The faces of Mathews and Drury are engraved on my brain, the cunning positively gleaming out of them ... but above all I remember the complacency of the three judges. Their general demeanour was like that of elderly club men determined that it should be clearly understood that they are men of the world, fully alive to all the tricks of your Tom, Dick and Harry, yet their actual questions and comments positively revealed that they had not the remotest notion of what sort of a world it was that these East End people they were listening to actually lived in.

(Coming himself from a working-class family in the East End Magee was well qualified to make this criticism.)

What later struck Ludo, reading the transcript, was the ludicrous incoherence of Mathews's evidence. For example, when asked by the defence counsel, David

McNeill, if he had thought it odd to be asked to go to Luton with three strangers in two other cars to pick up some parcels, he had replied:

> The only answer I can give to that is I did think it out and I when I did think it was something illegal I thought to myself 'why was I involved with the van and the car?' That was when we were in Luton, just entering Luton. My mind was carrying away through the streets I did not know, trying to memorise the way back. I could only say that I being an elderly person compared with these other three, it could be something illegal that they could put in my car. I did not know what and most likely the police seeing a person of my description would stop me if it was illegal. I did have that in mind.[76]

Anyone reading such a passage, and the other examples that Ludo gave, would dismiss it as gibberish but this was not the view that Messrs Roskill, Lawton and Wien took of Mathews: 'Each of us watched him closely while he was giving his evidence,' they wrote in their judgement. 'The conclusion which each of us independently has reached in this court of the vital part of his story is that he was clearly telling the truth.'[77]

Unlike the judges themselves, according to Magee:

---

[76] *Wicked Beyond Belief.*

[77] *Wicked Beyond Belief.*

The judges *did not* watch Mathews closely while he was giving evidence. I watched both them and Mathews closely throughout both days while he was giving evidence and for most of the time all three had their heads and eyes down on the notes they were keeping. Every now and then one of them would look up, but then almost always quickly back again ... over and again, when confronted with a crucial question, Mathews's face would be invaded by a shifty look, and he would turn his eyes away, and falter, and then visibly pull himself together and resume talking, but in a suddenly improvisatory tone of voice. Whenever this or anything like it happened, I always shot an immediate glance at the judges to see how they were reacting, only to find at least four times out of five that not a single one of them was looking at him.

The dismissal of yet another appeal, once again going against all the evidence, came as a devastating blow to Cooper and McMahon, not to mention Magee, who described feeling 'almost beside myself with frustration and rage'. But he did not abandon the campaign and wrote at length to Roy Jenkins, setting out a detailed criticism of the judgement and urging the Home Secretary to release the two men, as he was entitled to do. As it happened, Jenkins had only recently announced his intention to leave British politics and assume the presidency of the European Commission in Brussels, so he had nothing to lose by overruling the judges. But he refused, claiming that to do so would be insulting and a direct flouting of the court. So this urbane and clever man, much admired for his liberal instincts, showed himself in his last days in office to be weak and cowardly when faced with the opportunity to remedy a scandalous case of injustice, as he well knew it to be.

Jenkins's successor as Home Secretary, Merlyn Rees, a cautious and undistinguished figure, proved no more susceptible to Magee's arguments, despite the emergence of yet another witness for the defence. Nor, in July 1977, was he at all influenced by the sentencing to eight years imprisonment of Commander Drury for charges of corruption. During the trial, James Humphreys testified that he had paid Drury a total of at least £5,000 over the years, and that Drury had lived so well from free lunches and drinking sessions that the 'emperor of porn' had also met his request for slimming tablets and a rowing machine. Drury could only argue, like so many of his convicted colleagues at the time, that he was duty bound to associate with criminals in order to acquire valuable information. The conviction of Drury resulted in him being imprisoned in the same gaol, Wormwood Scrubs, in which David Cooper was serving out his even longer sentence. To add to this bizarre sequence of events, John Stonehouse, the former Postmaster General who had put up the £5,000 reward following the Luton murder, money entrusted to Drury to share out, had himself been sentenced to eight years the very next month after faking his suicide by drowning.

It was not until two years later in 1979 that an unexpected breakthrough finally came.

Hitherto Ludo had had no involvement in the Luton case, which was not surprising as he was caught up in the long, drawn-out campaign to release Patrick Meehan during the first half of the 1970s. Nor, when that miscarriage of justice was finally overturned in 1976, was he at all keen to take on another fight. So it was not with any great enthusiasm that he accepted delivery of a bulky parcel from his literary agent Michael Sissons at his Roxburghshire home. It was a handwritten manuscript by David Cooper that ran to 100,000 words. Cooper had passed it to Bryan Magee, who in turn had asked Sissons (his agent, too) to send it to Ludo. Magee cannot have had high hopes, as the book was not only long but shapeless and poorly written – not surprising in view of Cooper's very basic education.

Although the book was clearly unpublishable in its present form, Ludo was instantly convinced of Cooper's sincerity for the simple reason that he thought no one guilty of a crime would write so many words in order to assert his innocence. His feelings were confirmed when, on contacting McMahon's solicitor Wendy Mantle, he discovered that McMahon had written a similarly weighty tome, 'thankfully in typescript' – which left him in no doubt that he too was telling the truth and that he would never have written his book if he had been guilty. It was a natural and obvious reaction but one which would carry no weight at all in a court of law.

Ludo's response to the Luton story, as told by Cooper and McMahon and confirmed by talking to their solicitors Wendy Mantle and Gareth Peirce, was typical of the man. It was a tale, he wrote later, of 'wickedness and depravity hard to credit'.[78] In both the Evans and Meehan cases, Ludo had given the police the benefit of the doubt, accepting that if they had distorted or invented evidence, they had done so in the sincere belief that both men were guilty of murder. But here Commander Drury had known perfectly well that the three accused were innocent and that Mathews, the chief witness against them, was himself guilty of murder. Not only had Mathews walked free but he had, thanks to Drury, been financially rewarded by the State for his lies.

That was one part of the case. The other was the response of a series of Appeal Court judges (including the Lord Chief Justice), all of whom had adamantly refused to accept that Mathews was a liar, that Drury was corrupt, and that witnesses had been bribed with reward money.

---

[78] This and all other Ludo quotes relating to the Luton murder are from *Wicked Beyond Belief*.

With Cooper and McMahon now serving the ninth years of their sentences, Ludo felt that he needed to do whatever he could as quickly as possible. He arranged with his publisher, Mark Barty-King of Granada, that his book would be a paperback as this could be published more quickly. He also included extracts from Cooper's and McMahon's accounts as well as contributions from Peirce, Mantle, Thomson and Magee alongside his own narrative.

What gave the book an added authority was the involvement of Lord Devlin. Devlin, like many others, had been appalled by the outcome of the latest appeal case. On 2 May 1978, he had delivered two lectures at All Souls College, Oxford (following briefings by Magee and Peirce), in which he strongly criticised the Appeal Court judges for usurping the role of the jury. Encouraged by his friend Magee, he now agreed to contribute a chapter to Ludo's book, while expressing a typical lawyer's concern that everything in it should be carefully vetted by a libel lawyer. Hedging his criticisms with complimentary remarks about the judges – 'I have not the slightest doubt in the world about their anxiety to do justice' – and expressing his 'deep respect' (always a sign that what follows will demonstrate the exact opposite), Devlin moved towards a damning summing up:

Doubts do not just lurk:[79] from the first they have flown about the case like bats in a belfry. These men have now served more than half of the exemplary sentences passed on them. It is less than their deserts if they are guilty, but yet by any standard a drastic punishment. If they are innocent the thought of another ten years out of their lives is not tolerable. If the Home Secretary now cuts the knot, I do not believe that there is a voice in England that would be raised in protest.

By the time Ludo's book *Wicked Beyond Belief* came out in 1980 the Home Secretary was William Whitelaw, the Tories under Margaret Thatcher having been elected in May the previous year. Ludo had known Whitelaw since his childhood in Scotland; he also knew Thatcher's Lord Chancellor, Lord Hailsham, to whom he sent a copy of the book. Hailsham's permanent secretary was Ludo's cousin, Wilfred Bourne, who read the book and approached a senior Home Office civil servant, who in turn referred the matter to Whitelaw. A canny politician behind his rather bumbling façade, Whitelaw

---

[79] Bob Woffinden, *Miscarriages of Justice*, 1987. The reference to lurking doubts is a little legal dig directed at Lord Widgery, who coined the expression 'lurking doubt' as sufficient reason for allowing an appeal: 'The court must ask itself whether we are content to let the matter rest, or whether there is not some lurking doubt in our mind which makes us wonder whether an injustice has been done.' The expression was later current in the Court of Appeal. However, as the solicitor Sir David Napley pointed out, Widgery might have coined the phrase, 'but it was never as far as I could see a principle implemented by him'.

was aware of Ludo's influence and the likelihood that the case was never going to go away. He therefore gave orders that Cooper and McMahon should be released, announcing to the House of Commons: 'The case is wholly exceptional and I judge that there is a widely felt sense of unease about it. I share that unease. I have concluded that in view of my responsibility for the maintenance of public confidence in our system of criminal justice, the matter should now be resolved.'[80]

Seldom has a book achieved so dramatic a result in so short a time. 'It is a strange system,' a solicitor, Brian Raymond, wrote to *The Times*, 'that requires a paperback book to secure the release of an innocent man.'[81] Ludo's book was unlike its predecessors in that it contained contributions from others – the cover actually stated '*Edited* by Ludovic Kennedy' – but it was another example of how a coherent and, above all, well-written narrative could bring together and explain a string of events that had been spread over ten years. Reviewing it in the *Listener* on 10 July 1980, Tom Mangold wrote that after *Ten Rillington Place* and *Presumption of Innocence*, Ludo 'completes the hat-trick shattering the stumps that have held the prosecution innings together for over a decade . . . Kennedy's persistence, clear writing and organisation of complex

---

[80] Hansard.

[81] Bob Woffinden, *Miscarriages of* Justice, 1987.

material leaves most investigative reporters humbled.' Nobody had the tactlessness to mention the important role played in the denouement by the 'Old Boy Network', Ludo being on Christian-name terms with Whitelaw and Lord Lane, an acquaintance of fellow Old Etonian Lord Hailsham, while his cousin was Hailsham's permanent secretary.

Regrettably, Whitelaw's announcement was not to be the end of the story, for despite being released, Cooper and McMahon had not been given a free pardon and so, in the eyes of the law, they remained convicted murderers. This outcome provoked a number of protests, including a lengthy leader in *The Times*, with Ludo commenting, 'You can't keep men in prison for ten and a half years and then simply say maybe you have made a mistake and let them go.'[82]

Some years later, Ludo met Whitelaw when on holiday and asked him why a pardon had not been granted. 'I was all in favour,' Whitelaw replied, 'but Geoffrey Lane objected.' Lane – Lord Lane of St Ippolyts, in the county of Hertfordshire – had been appointed Lord Chief Justice in 1980 in succession to Lord Widgery, who, for some time, had been suffering from Parkinson's disease and accompanying dementia, prompting a scurrilous paragraph in *Private Eye* in September 1978: 'Lord Widgery was once an authority in his own court. Now he sits

---

[82] Bob Woffinden, *Miscarriages of Justice*, 1987.

hunched and scowling, squinting into his books from a range of three inches. He keeps up a muttered commentary of bad-tempered and irrelevant questions.'[83] Widgery's illness had been known to legal colleagues for some time but nothing had been done about it.

Born in 1918, the son of a Lincoln bank manager, Lane had been head boy at my own school, Shrewsbury. After 'a good war' in the RAF, he read law at Cambridge and was called to the Bar, becoming a judge in 1960. A quiet, unassuming character, Lane – along with Widgery and many other contemporaries – blotted his copybook when called upon to reach judgements in cases relating to the 'Troubles' in Northern Ireland. His darkest hour came in the 1988 appeal of the Birmingham Six (four of them represented by Gareth Peirce). In his judgement, Lane memorably pronounced: 'As with many cases referred by the Home Secretary to the Court of Appeal, the longer this case has gone on, the more convinced this court has become that the verdict of the jury was correct.'[84]

Lane was well known to Ludo. In 1965, he had acted as counsel for the police at Sir Daniel Brabin's inquiry into the Timothy Evans case, when Brabin had decided that Evans, though not guilty of murdering his baby

---

[83] This unflattering portrait was almost certainly the work of Bob Marshall-Andrews QC.

[84] Chris Mullin, *Error of Judgement: The Truth About the Birmingham Bombing*, 1986. Poolbeg.

daughter, had almost certainly murdered his wife. Lane had done his best on that occasion to rattle Ludo by accusing him of discussing the case with his counsel during the lunch break – something he was perfectly entitled to do. However, having read *Ten Rillington Place* very carefully, Lane must have been well aware of Ludo's abilities as an investigator. Besides which, he had considerable personal knowledge of the Luton case, having presided at three separate appeal hearings brought by some of those involved. The first was that of Michael Good, the owner of the gun that was used to shoot the postmaster (see page 150). Shortly after the murder, he had received a seven-year sentence for another post office robbery. But on appeal Lane and two other judges quashed the conviction.

Equally questionable was Lane's role in the case of Thomas Weyers, one of the two inmates of Leicester Prison who had submitted crucial evidence to the original trial – namely, that McMahon had given a detailed account of his involvement in the Luton raid. Weyers had later received a £500 reward for his information. When his own case went to appeal three months after McMahon was convicted, Lane and two colleagues reduced his thirty-three-month term of imprisonment to eighteen months and later to nine months, suspended for two years, while also announcing that Weyers was mentally unbalanced and in need of assistance and aftercare. Lane would not have liked it to be known that he had reduced Weyers's sentence to reward a mentally disturbed man who had been bribed by a senior police officer to commit perjury in a murder trial.

Lastly, in 1978 Lane ordered Ken Drury's sentence to be reduced from eight to five years, partly on the grounds that he had not corrupted any junior officers, a conclusion for which there was no proof and which was subsequently shown to be quite untrue. Like many policemen taking bribes from criminals, Drury was in the habit of passing on some of the money to his subordinates to make sure they were equally compromised.[85]

In urging Whitelaw not to grant Cooper and McMahon a free pardon, Lane may perhaps, as Ludo suggested, have been hoping to salvage the reputation of the Court of Appeal. But his Birmingham Six judgement, with its gratuitous reference to other unwarranted appeals – 'as with many cases referred by the Home Secretary to the Court of Appeal' – suggests an unwillingness to admit to any mistakes and the possibility that, after all that had happened in the Luton case, he was still prepared to assert the guilt of two innocent men.

Lane never recovered from his Birmingham Six judgement, which three years later resulted in 140 MPs

---

[85] CCRC Gareth Peirce submission. Former Detective Sergeant John Symonds said in a sworn statement: 'I have been asked whether it would be possible for any police officer who was a close associate of Drury's to have been completely honest ... The answer is that it would have been wholly impossible and Drury himself would not have ever allowed such a person near him.'

signing an early day motion demanding his resignation. Writing about the Birmingham judgement some years later – after Lane's verdict had been overturned – Ludo, who had been in court throughout, commented:

An expression of apology from Lord Lane . . . [and his colleagues] for their previous cock-up would not have come amiss but that is not the English way . . . [Lane] gave no indication that he intended to do anything but stay where he was and would presumably have thought any sort of apology or expression of regret for his and his colleagues' ineptitude *infra dig*. Yet one cannot think of any other profession or business where, had the managing director been found guilty of similar incompetence (in this instance leading to a further three years' imprisonment of six innocent men) he would not have been faced with a call for his immediate resignation or dismissal.[86]

As so often, Ludo could deflect any accusations of malice on his part by speaking affectionately of Lane, whom he had met some years previously at a lawyers' conference in Aviemore. They became friends, he wrote, and 'played the odd round of golf together'.[87] Lane, however, like so many judges, strongly resented any criticism from outsiders, particularly journalists. Following the

---

[86] *Thirty-six Murders and Two Immoral Earnings.*

[87] *Thirty-six Murders and Two Immoral Earnings.*

Birmingham Six appeal, Ludo called for his resignation, telling the *Sunday Times* on 29 May 1991, 'Professionally I think he's a disaster.' Lane severed their relationship immediately. By contrast, Ludo would probably have been quite happy to go on playing golf with Lane. 'My criticism is purely professional,' he told the paper.

Ludo's title for his book, *Wicked Beyond Belief*, was a quotation from Mr Justice Cusack's summing up in Murphy, Cooper and McMahon's original Old Bailey trial in March 1970, when the judge had declared, 'To involve three innocent men in this way would surely be wicked beyond belief.' In other words, it was simply not credible that Mathews had deliberately framed the defendants. Thereafter, over the next decade, campaigners for justice and Appeal Court judges alike would come up against this problem time and again. There was another difficulty, too, particularly for the judges, with their reluctance to think ill of the police. If you accepted that Mathews had given false evidence to convict the three men, it followed that he must have done so with the connivance of Drury, who was, at the time of the first Luton trial, a well-respected police officer with a long and successful career behind him. But since his resignation and subsequent imprisonment for corruption it was easier to accept that, if anyone was 'wicked beyond belief', it was Drury himself – the man who had masterminded the conspiracy.

Even so, Ludo was severely hampered in 1980 – the year in which his book was published – by the fact that Drury was still alive. Even though he had already served a lengthy prison sentence, Ludo's publishers and their legal advisers would have viewed his involvement in the Luton case with trepidation, particularly as Lord Devlin, in giving the book his imprimatur, was so anxious that there should be no legal repercussions. So, in spite of all that had emerged, Ludo was unable to spell out the obvious truth that Drury and Mathews had colluded to incriminate Murphy, Cooper and McMahon. 'Suggestions have been made as to the possibilities of collusion,' he wrote apropos Mathews's patently invented story of his trip to Luton to pick up a parcel. 'Collusion cannot be ruled out.' As for the suggestion that Drury had pocketed some of the reward money, Ludo was advised to write to the ex-commander's solicitor, who unsurprisingly rejected the notion, leaving Ludo to reach the distinctly lame conclusion that 'his denials regarding the reward money cannot be accepted as proof positive'.

Drury, who had served most of his sentence in an open prison, was released on parole in September 1979. He continued to assert his innocence, telling the *Daily Mail* on 4 September 1979, 'As a policeman it was essential that I mixed with known criminals,' and pledging that he would appeal to the European Commission for Human Rights in order to clear his name (he never did). He returned to his home in Sidcup, but the following year, when Cooper and McMahon were finally released, perhaps fearing that he might be rearrested or even become the victim of a revenge attack, he disappeared, only re-emerging when it became clear that there would not be an enquiry let alone a police investigation. He died of a heart attack in 1984, at the age of sixty-two. Brief press reports recalled the Humphreys affair. There was no reference to Luton.

The danger of forming close links with criminals was that they could turn very nasty, should you fall out with them. In Drury's case, this had happened with James Humphreys, the notorious 'emperor of porn' who had once been so close to him. When their relationship became public knowledge, Humphreys was desperate to put distance between himself and Drury because of the risks associated with being a known police informer. Jailed himself for shooting and wounding his wife Rusty's lover in 1974, Humphreys was quite happy to give evidence against Drury at the latter's trial, and was guaranteed remission as a result. He subsequently made a statement for Gareth Peirce 'to the effect that a number of decisions had had to be made in the [Luton] case because of the involvement in the murder of an informant of the Flying Squad and the subsequent threat *that difficulties would be raised about the Flying Squad*'.[88]

---

[88] Submission to the Criminal Cases Review Commission, May 2000 (emphasis added).

Humphreys, who had spoken to Drury several times about the Luton case and was generally reliable, partly because he kept a diary, named the informant as Mathews – plainly a mistake as Mathews was far too unreliable and incoherent a character to be of much use to the police. (It is equally possible that Drury deliberately misled Humphreys, as he wished to protect the identity of the real informant.) The man he should and could have named was one Michael Good, a reliable informant for one of Drury's subordinates, Detective Sergeant Fallon of the Flying Squad. During the Old Bailey trial, Good, who had almost certainly been a member of the Luton gang along with Mathews, had given evidence about the gun used to kill Mr Stevens. Drury knew this evidence to be false, yet Good, like Mathews, was granted immunity from prosecution on account of his cooperation. It eventually transpired that it was Good, via DS Fallon, who had provided the police with the names of Murphy, Cooper and McMahon. He had previously checked that McMahon would be able to produce only a 'family alibi' prior to his arrest and the impression was spread by police that at the time of the crime he himself had been in prison – which was not the case.

For his assistance, Good received £500 of the reward money, which he passed straight back to Drury. This was surely part of his deal with the police chief, who had guaranteed Good's protection in exchange for his silence and continued cooperation. According to

Humphreys, Good had made it clear that he could create 'difficulties' for Drury and the Flying Squad, though he never explicitly stated what those difficulties might be.

When this elaborate conspiracy was finally unravelled, one question became paramount. Why did Commander Ken Drury, who had at least two of the Luton gang (Mathews and Good) bang to rights, engage in an elaborate and risky conspiracy to protect them and convict three innocent men of the murder in their stead? In his book *Miscarriages of Justice* (1987), Bob Woffinden advances the theory that Drury himself 'set up' the Luton raid. Humphreys had hinted as much, and McMahon's MP, Dr Oonagh McDonald, raised the possibility in the House of Commons. It seems unlikely, however, that Drury, admittedly not a very clever man, would have been so foolish as to enlist the volatile Mathews to take part in an armed robbery whatever the nature of his involvement.

In a long and revealing affidavit written to assist Gareth Peirce in her submission to the Criminal Cases Review Commission in 2000,[89] a former associate of Drury – one-time Detective Sergeant John Symonds – gave an account of the commander's methods.[90] He

---

[89] The Criminal Appeal Act of 1997 established the CCRC as an independent body to review possible miscarriages of justice and refer appropriate cases to the appeal courts.

[90] Symonds was not involved in the Luton case himself.

explained that Drury was a forceful and domineering man, known to colleagues as 'Trumpet' because of his loud voice, who had little time for conventional detective work. 'He was obsessed with acquiring information from informants,' Symonds stated. 'In my experience he would take information from informants and would make the case fit what he had been told.' So was Drury's inclination to accommodate Good when he provided the names of Murphy, Cooper and McMahon in relation to the Luton murder? And did he then persuade Mathews to incriminate the three men – as there was no other evidence against them – in order to secure a conviction and leave the informer Good out of the equation altogether?

Good, we know, gave his £500 share of the reward to Drury as a small price to pay for avoiding a murder charge. But Drury will have been aware of the need to keep Good sweet and so avoid any of the unnamed 'difficulties' to which Humphreys referred. Early in his career, Symonds said, Drury would regularly bring Symonds with him when he went to the West End to meet the powerful gangsters who supplied the commander with information in exchange for immunity:

I would take him, and be with him when he talked to his informants. My presence would be useful in more than one way, not simply to drive him and be a companion, but in view of the fact that he was meeting with and consorting with dangerous people both physically and intimidatory in many cases but importantly cunning people, and consequently my presence would be both physical protection potentially and a back-up lest anyone tried to, in turn, fit him up.

This was a forceful indication that Drury was well aware of the dangers of relying on criminals for his results.

Given all of the risks involved, Drury must have been amazed by the astonishing success of his frame-up, which was upheld first by the Old Bailey jury and then by a record number of Appeal Court judges, despite the growing mountain of evidence against it. All this was in marked contrast to the raid itself, which had been hopelessly bungled and chaotic.

Ludo did not lose interest in Cooper and McMahon following their release in 1980. Thus, three years later, along with Bryan Magee and Roy Jenkins – anxious perhaps to make amends for his failure to intervene in 1977 – he petitioned the new Home Secretary, Leon Brittan, to grant a pardon. Brittan, typically, expressed his sympathy but then did nothing.

Meanwhile, Ludo followed up the story of Thomas Weyers, one of the two witnesses who were fellow prisoners of McMahon prior to his trial and who had given evidence at Luton that he had confessed to the murder from his adjoining cell. After reading *Wicked*

Beyond Belief, Weyers was overcome with remorse and wrote to Ludo, offering to make a statement in which he would admit to lying under oath. He would come to London, he said, if Ludo would pay his travel expenses and hotel bill. Ludo agreed. In his statement to Ludo, Weyers described being visited by one of Drury's subordinates, Horn, who visited him in prison and related what Drury wanted him to say. He had also promised some of the reward money. After the trial, Weyers learned that Drury was pleased with him and that he was not to worry about his sentence because the Commander would 'put in a good word for him'. Sure enough, when Weyers's case came before the Appeal Court judges, one of whom was Geoffrey Lane, his sentence, originally thirty-three months, was reduced to nine months, suspended for two years, and he was immediately released. The CCRC submission of 2000 stated that the judges were 'very guarded in their reasons for reducing the sentence' to which Ludo commented, 'I bet they were.'[91]

It was not until August 2003 that the Court of Appeal, in response to Gareth Peirce's submission to the CCRC, finally quashed Cooper's and McMahon's convictions. Thirty-four years had gone by since the murder of postmaster Reginald Stevens. Cooper had died in 1993, aged fifty-one, and McMahon six years later, on his

---

[91] *Thirty-six Murders and Two Immoral Earnings*.

fifty-fifth birthday. Neither had received a penny in compensation. Gareth stated in her submission to the CCRC: 'The writer of these submissions has no doubt that the life and health of each was drastically affected by the eleven years each spent in torment in prison.'

Drury and Mathews had both died without being held to account for their crimes. No attempt was made to recover the reward money paid to those who had given false witness. Four Home Secretaries and ten Appeal Court judges (including two Lord Chief Justices) had been implicated in the case. But no judge and no politician apologised to the families of the wrongly convicted men. Although Mathews and Good were named as probable members of the Luton gang, they escaped scot-free; the other two were never identified.

It all added up to one of the most scandalous and discreditable cases in the history of British justice. Yet there was little interest in the 2003 Appeal Court hearing, attended as it was by those few campaigners who had fought so long to clear the names of Cooper and McMahon, both of them now dead. Ludo himself, aged eighty-three and walking with the help of a stick, sat in the court among them. At one stage, when the barrister representing the CCRC was ploughing through the evidence, he remarked very audibly, 'How much longer is he going on?'

'To think of all those wasted lives,' said Gareth Peirce, echoing Mr Justice Cusack. 'It's tragic and cruel and wrong beyond belief.'[92] In Ludo's book, Bryan Magee had written: 'We ought none of us to lose sight of the fact that human beings count for more than institutions or procedures or precedents and we ought always to be willing, given justification, to sacrifice the latter to the former.'

---

[92] *Guardian*, 1 August 2003.

Chapter 4

Richard Hauptmann

'I hope to God this is the last book I write that tries to right a legal wrong,' Ludo told the *Sunday People* (date unknown) after the success of *Wicked Beyond Belief*. He had said the same sort of thing when *A Presumption of Innocence* – the story of Paddy Meehan – had been published four years earlier. He knew the amount of work involved and all the frustration that lies in store for anyone who gets involved with the law and lawyers. But at the same time he was only too aware of the irresistible pull that could, at any time, drag him back to what he was best at. 'These books force themselves upon me,' he said.

In the meantime, he had a score or so of television projects to occupy him. Throughout the 1970s, he had produced a series of documentaries for the BBC about the naval battles of the Second World War. They included, most memorably, a gripping account of the sinking of the *Bismarck* in 1941, a battle in which Ludo himself had played a small part. Typically for

Ludo, it avoided anything in the nature of patriotic flag-waving and gave equal prominence to some of the German survivors, including Baron von Müllenheim-Rechberg, who was on the *Scharnhorst* when it sank Ludo's father's ship, the *Rawalpindi*. There was no film of the battle, so the programme relied on what TV people call, disparagingly, 'talking heads', survivors from both sides telling their stories directly to camera, with Ludo himself (the interviewer) remaining out of shot. Most memorable was the actor Esmond Knight, who described how he had been blinded in the battle.[93]

Another nautical assignment came Ludo's way when he was asked to make an obituary programme for Lord Mountbatten. It was an unusual commission as Mountbatten wished to appear in it and give directions for his funeral – those hymns and readings he wished to be used. Ludo, who liked and admired Mountbatten, had met him previously in 1975, when they had both been guest speakers at a naval dinner in Newcastle. He remembered arranging to meet the Admiral at his hotel and, finding his room open, witnessed the unusual sight of Mountbatten sitting in his shirt sleeves in front of the mirror while his ADC knelt on the floor behind him, brushing the curls at the back of his head.

---

[93] Coincidentally, Knight appeared with Moira Shearer in *The Red Shoes* after the war.

After Mountbatten was murdered by the IRA in August 1979, Ludo's obituary programme was shown twice. As television critic of the *Spectator* at the time, I reviewed it rather disparagingly, accusing Ludo of obsequiousness and Mountbatten himself of outrageous self-regard, convinced of the success of all his actions. (In the documentary, he brushed aside the slaughter that followed his partition of India by saying that, while 200,000 people were killed, this was a tiny percentage of a population of 400 million.) As so often, however, God was not mocked. Not content with arranging his own funeral, Mountbatten seemed to think he could equally well arrange his own death, telling Ludo, 'I'm going to enjoy the fun of dying. I don't mind when it comes so long as it's a reasonably peaceful and satisfying death.' Rather surprisingly, in view of the horrible circumstances of his actual death, the BBC did not edit this out when the programme was broadcast.

Shortly after Mountbatten's death, his executors, headed by his son-in-law Lord Brabourne, set about looking for a suitable person to write his authorised biography and Ludo eagerly put his name forward. His naval experience in the war and his work on the obituary programme would, he felt, recommend him to the executors. But it was not to be. For whatever reason, he was passed over and the job went instead to Philip

Ziegler, Ludo's editor at Collins.[94] Ludo was no doubt disappointed, but from his point of view the choice of Ziegler was fortunate. Writing Mountbatten's life would have been a colossal task likely to have taken him four or five years, involving foreign travel and a massive amount of research. Had he been commissioned, it is most unlikely that he would ever have written what was to be his longest, most ambitious and most gripping book about a miscarriage of justice – *The Airman and the Carpenter.*

In 1980 Will Wyatt, the assistant head of the BBC's Presentation Department, conceived the idea of a weekly critical programme about television. Lasting for half an hour on Sunday evenings, the idea behind it was to involve three different guests, each of whom would speak about a programme they had watched in the past week. The novelist Susan Hill was initially chosen to chair the programme, to be called *Did You See?*, but she failed to impress and Ludo, considered by Wyatt to be 'a jolly nice person to have in your sitting room on a Sunday evening, someone with a slightly patrician but mischievous manner',[95] was given the job. He proved to be the ideal chairman, a role he performed regularly for the next eight years.

---

[94] Significantly, perhaps, when his book was published, Ziegler glossed over the allegations of Mountbatten's homosexuality. I raised this issue in *Private Eye* after the Admiral's death, and Ludo might well have felt the need to address it if he had received the commission.

[95] Interview with author.

It was in the early days of *Did You See?* that Ludo flew to New York to film a couple of interviews for the programme, and it was there that, once again, he experienced a summons that he was unable to resist:

The place was my hotel bedroom, the time around 8 a.m. As one often does in New York, I was flicking through the television channels while awaiting the arrival of orange juice and coffee. I did not know what channel I was tuned to when there swam into my vision a very old lady proclaiming with vehemence that her husband was innocent of the crime of which he had been convicted. I sat up and paid attention for this was, as it were, my territory ... then slowly it dawned on me – for the scene had been set before I tuned in – that the old lady was none other than Anna Hauptmann, the widow of Richard Hauptmann, the German immigrant who had been executed by the state of New Jersey in 1936 for the kidnapping and murder of the baby son of Charles Lindbergh.[96]

And then Ludo remembered from his schooldays a photograph – rather like the one of Timothy Evans at Paddington Station – 'a picture that would be seared on my mind for ever, a full-page photograph of the haunted, unshaven face of Richard Hauptmann as it

---

[96] This and all subsequent Ludo quotes relating to the Lindbergh case are from *The Airman and the Carpenter* and his BBC film.

first appeared after his arrest and, then again, on the day of his electrocution two years later'.

As with the chance meeting with Nicholas Fairbairn and their conversation on a train the night before Paddy Meehan was convicted of murder and sentenced to life imprisonment, Ludo experienced a surge of adrenalin. It was not just the assurance and confidence with which Anna Hauptmann, in her marked German accent, spoke, but also her dignity and strong sense of right and wrong. Would an old lady of eighty-nine, whose husband had been executed nearly half a century ear-lier, continue to campaign on his behalf and travel all the way to New York to appear on television to make the case if she knew – or even suspected – him to be guilty? To Ludo, it was inconceivable, just as it had been inconceivable that David Cooper would write a 100,000-word book proclaiming his innocence if he had murdered Reginald Stevens.

So, on the basis of one brief glimpse of part of a TV interview in a hotel bedroom, Ludo embarked immediately on yet another crusade. But this one was in quite a different league from those that had gone before. This was not Notting Hill, Glasgow or Luton but the United States, and he would be investigating a killing that had taken place in March 1932 – a mur-der that had aroused worldwide interest and inspired thousands of pages of press coverage, not to mention several books.

The basic story, familiar still to most Americans in the 1980s, was easily told on 1 March 1932. Charlie, the twenty-month-old son of the aviator Charles Lindbergh – internationally famous on account of his solo flight across the Atlantic in 1929 – was abducted from his cot in the family home at Hopewell, New Jersey. Lindbergh received a ransom demand and handed over $50,000 to men claiming to be the kidnappers. However, two months later, Charlie's body was found in nearby woodland. Finally, following an investigation that lasted more than two years, some of the ransom money was traced to a German-born carpenter, Richard Hauptmann, who was tried, found guilty and executed in 1936. In the eyes of almost all who had followed the story, justice had been done.

On his return to London, Ludo applied to the BBC's Will Wyatt, the man who had launched him on *Did You See?* and a keen admirer of his talents, to produce a documentary on the Lindbergh kidnapping. Wyatt agreed and gave him a whole year in which to make the film, having first assigned a young and very energetic producer, Sue Crowther, to work with him. It was a shrewd move and the two quickly formed a good working relationship and respect for one another's abilities.

There was a massive amount of research for Sue Crowther to do. The New Jersey police had, in response to a demand by Anna Hauptmann's lawyer, recently released the Lindbergh files containing all the evidence relating to the trial. It was this that had brought the elderly Anna to New York for her TV appearance. In addition to the files and reams of newspaper clippings, numerous books on the case had been published since 1932. The Lindbergh kidnapping, like the assassination of President Kennedy three decades later, had given rise to a score or so of conspiracy theories which had managed to spread a fog of fantasy and wild speculation over the case. If Hauptmann was guilty, as most people accepted, then he could not have acted alone, so who were his accomplices? If he was innocent, who was guilty? It was here that the theorists' imaginations ran riot. Shortly after the baby's body was discovered, rumours had begun to circulate that the Lindberghs themselves had killed Charlie because he was either mentally handicapped or deformed. Then a Chicago lawyer wrote a pamphlet suggesting that Charlie had never been kidnapped at all; rather, he had simply wandered off into the woods and died.

There were plenty of leads for amateur sleuths to follow up: how did the kidnappers know that the Lindbergh family would be in residence, which they never normally were on Tuesday night? Why had they chosen a time early in the evening when the Lindberghs were up and about? There was even an echo of Sherlock Holmes's 'curious incident of the dog in the night-time' – the Lindberghs's dog having failed to bark at the intruders. Then there was the mysterious suicide of Violet Sharpe, an English girl from Tutts Clump in Berkshire who had been working in Mrs Lindbergh's parents' house at the time of the kidnapping. She swallowed cyanide-chloride silver polish after aggressive questioning by the police (nothing was ever proved against her).

Even after Ludo's programme and subsequent book, the wild conspiracy theories continued to appear, as if there were something irresistibly fascinating about the story for amateur detectives and crime novelists. In 1993 a book by Gregory Ahlgren and Stephen Monier even proposed that Lindbergh himself, well known as a practical joker, had staged the kidnapping to give his wife a scare and had accidentally killed his baby in the attempt. A year later, in 1994, another book by crime writer Noel Behn accused Anne Lindbergh's elder sister Elizabeth, who was known to have mental problems, of the killing. She had, Behn claimed, been in love with Lindbergh and had thrown the baby out of the window in a fit of jealous rage. Perhaps the most fanciful of all, *In Search of the Lindbergh Baby* (1981) by Theon Wright advanced the theory that the body found in the woods was not that of Charlie Lindbergh and that he was still alive in the person of one Harold Olson. (As Ludo pointed out in an appendix to his own book, Wright failed to appreciate that if this theory were true, there must have been two kidnappings, not just one.)

Sue Crowther was keen for Ludo to look into some of the more plausible theories. After all, if they were both convinced of Hauptmann's innocence, wasn't it logical to try to identify the guilty party or parties? Ludo however was adamant that he would not go down that path. Despite the fact that Crowther titled their film (eventually shown in 1982) *Who Killed the Lindbergh Baby?*, it made little or no attempt to answer the question. With his storyteller's instinct, Ludo sensed that the interest lay not in speculative detective work, but rather, as it had done in the story of Rillington Place, with the tragic tale of an innocent man caught up in a nightmare which ended in his death by execution. In this story Hauptmann was the hero and his wife Anna the heroine while the 'national hero' Lindbergh, who had helped the authorities to convict him, was left diminished and discredited. It was a topsy-turvy version of events but a true one, and one that in the end was too much for the American public to accept.

Ludo knew that if he was to investigate the story thoroughly he would have to write a book about it, a book that would inevitably be longer than anything he had previously written. In contrast, the commentary of an hour-long TV programme would amount to only 7,000 words and, as he always maintained, the impact of television was negligible. However well made a programme, it would be half-forgotten the day after. Yet to compress the Lindbergh story into one hour of television represented a challenge that Ludo could not resist. And he was pleasantly surprised at the outset to discover how many of those involved were still both alive and willing to be interviewed – Anna Hauptmann most notably, but also two of Hauptmann's closest friends, his fellow-carpenter Hans Kloppenburg, a policeman who had discovered a crucial piece of evidence and even a member of the jury that had found Hauptmann guilty. However, as the BBC stated in their press release prior to the broadcast, 'family and friends of the Lindberghs were approached but declined to take part'. Ludo was naturally disappointed that Lindbergh's widow Anne, whom he admired, was unwilling to be interviewed, though she did reply to his request saying that if there had been injustice then it was right that it should be exposed.

Not only had many witnesses survived, but the buildings where the main scenes of the drama had been acted out were still standing, showing remarkably little alteration – not just the Lindbergh house at Hopewell but the Hauptmanns' flat in New York, the attic from which he had allegedly taken part of the floorboard when making the ladder found outside the baby's window and the little courthouse at Flemington, New Jersey. Even Hauptmann's cell on death row at Trenton remained, and was visited by Ludo in the course of his researches – 'Today the death house in Trenton is no longer in use: but along the length of its empty, echoing cells, in the dust that accumulates daily on the unswept floors, in the abandoned electrocution chamber where the outline of the chair, like some obscene footprint disfigures the wall, there is still the smell of death.'

The story, unlike the sinking of the *Bismarck*, had been recorded from beginning to end on newsreel film. So *Who Killed the Lindbergh Baby?* opened with shots of the aviator's famous flight across the Atlantic in his tiny biplane, *The Spirit of St Louis*, the crowds who greeted him in Paris, and his subsequent tour around the world, including the ticker-tape parade through New York – Lindbergh, a gangling, boyish six-footer, shy but smiling, bemused by his sudden celebrity. There was also footage of him with his fiancée, Anne Morrow, the petite, bookish daughter of the banker Dwight Morrow, one of the richest men in America, by now the US Ambassador to Mexico. Ludo and his team visited the young couple's house at Hopewell, sixty miles from the Morrows' luxurious mansion at Englewood. Standing in dark woodland, the house, which had since become a children's home, had an abandoned, half-finished look, but the layout was unchanged from half a century earlier. Ludo's viewers could see the baby's bedroom and Lindbergh's study below, where he was reading when the Scottish nanny Betty Gow discovered – to her horror – that Charlie's crib was empty. There followed predictable footage of the nationwide hue-and-cry, along with images of hundreds of police searching the grounds and press reporters, almost invariably wearing hats, phoning through their copy, which was making headlines all over the world.

Lindbergh's prestige was such that he was able to take charge of the search himself, and when he received several notes demanding money for Charlie's return he ordered the police to stay out of the negotiations. Instead, he recruited a cranky intermediary by the name of Dr John Condon to make contact with those claiming to be the kidnappers.[97] The ransom money, $50,000, was handed over outside a New York cemetery on the night of 2 April, but six weeks later Charlie's mutilated body was found half-buried in the woods five miles from the Lindberghs' home.

It was two years later that some of the bills (whose serial numbers had been recorded) were traced to the German-born carpenter Richard Hauptmann, who was arrested, charged with murder and from then on assumed by police, press and public to be guilty of kidnap and murder. But, once again, as with Timothy Evans, the all-important question was being overlooked and went on being overlooked long after Hauptmann's execution: quite apart from any evidence, in the light of what was known about him, was he the sort of man who would single-handedly kidnap (and kill) a twenty-month-old baby in the hope of extorting a small fortune in ransom money?

---

[97] Lindbergh described Condon as an 'old and kindly professor from the Bronx'. Ludo called him 'a publicity-seeking, garrulous old bore'.

A refugee from the postwar Germany of shortages and inflation, Hauptmann, the son of a stonemason, had been wounded in the First World War and later served a thirty-month jail sentence for accosting two women in the street and stealing food and money at gunpoint. A second prison sentence for further thefts followed, after which Hauptmann promised his mother, a devout Lutheran, that he would go straight. Along with many of his countrymen in the 1920s, a period of economic meltdown in Germany, he determined to emigrate to America. After two unsuccessful attempts as a stowaway, he eventually walked ashore at Hoboken, New Jersey, after ten days of hiding in a steamer's coal bunkers. On landing, he thanked God for his good fortune. It was one of many ironies in the story that the country in which Richard Hauptmann had so desperately sought refuge would later prove his destroyer.

Anna Schoeffler had been in America for only three months when she met Hauptmann in 1924. Two years later, they were married. By now, Hauptmann, who had trained as a carpenter in Germany, was in regular employment, while Anna worked first as a waitress and then in a bakery. They soon saved enough money to rent an apartment in Park Avenue, and were even able to explore the Rockies and the West Coast by car with a group of fellow German friends. Their only child, Manfred, was born in 1933. By then a respectable bourgeois couple, the Hauptmanns were regular members of the congregation at St Paul's Lutheran church on 156th Street.

Although the trial was filmed, the courtroom scenes revealed little about Hauptmann. He remained seated throughout, wooden, impassive and smartly dressed, showing no sign of the effects of his weeks in solitary confinement, while the prosecuting counsel, David T. Wilentz, his voice rising and gesticulating with stiffened arms like a puppet, tried to break him down and make him admit to the crime. But either Hauptmann was mad or he was so sure of his innocence that he was able to distance himself from the drama about him and patiently sit and wait for the truth to emerge. This was certainly the attitude of Anna Hauptmann, who told Ludo in her broken English, 'Before the trial and after the trial I know something must happen – that Richard can come home – but nobody came forward.'[98] Several years later, Ludo wrote: 'I do not know of any woman whose integrity and strength of character I have admired more. During our many meetings she was calm, constant, resolute: sad and uncomprehending but never bitter.'[99] Filmed for his TV programme, she was handicapped by her strong German accent which made her,

---

[98] This seems to be a common reaction among those accused of crimes they have not committed. For instance, Hugh Callaghan, one of the Birmingham Six, said: 'During the trial I always firmly believed that something would show up' (interview by Naim Attallah for *The Oldie*, 1994).

[99] *Independent Magazine*, 3 December 1988.

at times, difficult to follow but there was quite enough evidence to support Ludo's very striking tribute – her dignity, her conviction and, above all, her strong moral sense shone through. Hauptmann's defence counsel, Edward Reilly, she said, wanted her to confirm Hauptmann's story that his friend Isidor Fisch had brought the ransom money to their house in a shoebox for safe-keeping. 'When he said that I was shocked. He's my lawyer and he wanted me to lie and I said, "Mr Reilly, you want me to *lie*!" and I looked at him and I said, "I am going on the witness stand and when I go there I want to tell the truth, because the jury would see that I am lying, the church, everybody would see that I am lying."'

Perhaps it is too much to say that everybody who saw her on TV knew that Anna Hauptmann was telling the truth. But it was hard for the viewer not to have the same reaction as Ludo in his hotel bedroom – that here was an old lady speaking with fierce conviction. Was it remotely possible that she was completely unaware that she had been married to a child kidnapper and killer? Equally, was it possible that she could continue to tell the same lie so convincingly for half a century?

On the other hand, if she was telling the truth, and Richard Hauptmann was innocent, all of the key witnesses at his trial must have lied, including Charles Lindbergh himself. Most Americans found it difficult to contemplate this logic. Many still do, even today.

With his knowledge of the Timothy Evans case (not to mention Paddy Meehan and the Luton post office murder), Ludo had no difficulty with the notion of a trumped-up case ending in the conviction of an innocent man. The difference here was that the injustice had been done quite openly and witnessed by readers and viewers all over the world. Ford Madox Ford, Damon Runyon and Edna Ferber were among the four hundred or so journalists who attended the so-called 'Trial of the Century' in the crowded courtroom at Flemington, New Jersey. The proceedings were also captured on newsreel film, which conveyed the almost carnival atmosphere – the souvenir sellers, the crowds milling around outside, all hoping to catch a glimpse of Hauptmann and his accuser, Lindbergh. The outcome seemed inevitable as witness after witness pointed an accusing finger at the accused man. If told that they were witnessing one of the most outrageous miscarriages of justice in history, they would have greeted the news with incredulity.

But by the time Ludo came to make his film and later to write his book, conditions were a little more favourable for anyone wishing to challenge the consensus. In 1977 an American journalist, Anthony Scaduto, who had gained access to police files and interviewed a number of key figures, including Anna Hauptmann and prosecuting counsel David Wilentz, published a book entitled *Scapegoat*. This offered the first detailed analysis of the evidence against Hauptmann and showed that almost all of it was deeply suspect. Most damning of all was Scaduto's discovery that payroll records showing that Hauptmann had been working all day on construction at the Majestic Apartments on 72nd Street on 1 March 1932 (the day of the kidnap) had gone missing. There was, however, proof in the files that the records *had* existed, and that the supervisor on the building site, J. M. Furcht, had originally sworn an affidavit confirming that Hauptmann had worked that day but had subsequently been persuaded to retract his evidence by the police.

When writing his book some years later, Ludo was bound to go over the same ground and repeat some of Scaduto's findings, but his main aim was rather different. He certainly did not want to follow Scaduto's example and be diverted into speculation about who the real kidnappers were.[100] Nor was it simply a case of championing the cause of Anna Hauptmann. As in the Meehan case, when Ludo had confessed to a fascination with all of the principal characters, here his storyteller's instinct drew him towards the drama of two men – Hauptmann, a German immigrant, and Lindbergh,

---

[100] Scaduto named one Paul Wendel as the kidnapper and speculated that Lindbergh connived in Hauptmann's conviction for the peace of mind of his wife in order 'to close out this case and this tormenting period of their lives'. He also subscribed to the theory that the body found in the woods was not that of Charlie Lindbergh.

the grandson of a Swedish immigrant – both of them married to devoted, God-fearing wives. To illustrate the similarity, Ludo juxtaposed two photographs: on the left, Hauptmann, smart and dignified in a dark suit, his hand on the shoulder of Anna, who sits demurely at his side, with hands folded on her lap; on the right, Lindbergh and Anne, her hands likewise folded, standing beside a plane. Both pictures suggest two very devoted couples at ease in one another's company.

The first of these pictures posed a challenge to those who upheld and defended the jury's verdict and the execution of Richard Hauptmann. In defiance of what looked like bourgeois domestic respectability, they were obliged to turn him into a monster. Just as John Eddowes dubbed poor Timothy Evans a dangerous psychopath, Jim Fisher, a one-time FBI agent turned Professor of Criminal Justice, labelled Hauptmann 'not legally insane . . . but he was defective and incomplete as a human. On the surface, Hauptmann looked and behaved like an ordinary man but beneath the façade there was no conscience, no insight, no imagination, no perception and no feelings except greed and anger.'[101] For good measure, Fisher quoted the opinion of a fellow FBI agent, who claimed that Hauptmann, with whom he had spent some time, had 'a low bovine mentality'.[102]

---

[101] J. Fisher, *The Lindbergh Case*, 1987.

[102] J. Fisher, *The Lindbergh Case*, 1987.

Lindbergh himself describes Hauptmann in similar terms, as recorded by the British diplomat and author Harold Nicolson, who was staying at Hopewell at the time of the trial, researching his biography of Dwight Morrow, Lindbergh's father-in-law. Nicolson writes in his diary on 14 February 1933, the day of the verdict:

After dinner we went into the library and the wireless was on in the dining room next door . . . We discussed Dwight for some twenty minutes. Suddenly Betty put her head round the huge coromandel screen. She looked very white. 'Hauptmann,' she said, 'has been condemned to death without mercy.'

We went into the drawing room. The wireless had been turned on to the scene outside the courthouse. One could hear the almost diabolic yelling of the crowd. They were all sitting round – Miss Morgan with her embroidery, Anne looking very white and still. 'You now heard,' broke in the voice of the announcer, 'the verdict in the most famous trial in all history. Bruno Hauptmann now stands guilty of the foulest . . .' 'Turn that off, Charles, turn that off.' Then we went into the pantry and had ginger beer.

Poor Anne – she looks so white and horrified. The yells of the crowd were really terrifying. 'That,' said Lindbergh, 'was a lynching crowd.' He tells me that Hauptmann was a magnificent looking man. Splendidly built, but that his little eyes were like the eyes of a wild boar. Mean, shifty, small and cruel.[103] No one who watched Ludo's film, with its many close-ups of Hauptmann during and after the trial, would recognise that description, which merely suggests that Lindbergh managed to convince himself that he helped to convict a guilty man who was deserving of execution. (How otherwise could he live out the rest of his life, if troubled by doubts that he had played a key role in sending an innocent man to the electric chair?)

Ever since Hauptmann's arrest, scores of journalists, with the help of the police, had been searching for information about him from every possible source. But the sad fact was that there was nothing at all to support the Fisher/Lindbergh picture of Hauptmann as mean and cruel, let alone a defective human being or a wild boar. His old friend and fellow carpenter Hans Kloppenburg, whom Ludo interviewed at length and who appeared on his BBC film, described a closely-knit group of German immigrants of whom he was one – like the Hauptmanns he still spoke with a pronounced accent – who socialised and even holidayed together. He himself had, he said, enjoyed regular musical evenings, singing German songs, with Kloppenburg on guitar and Hauptmann playing the mandolin. Like Anna, Kloppenburg stressed Hauptmann's love of nature and walking in the countryside.

---

[103] *Harold Nicolson Diaries and Letters, 1930–1939*. Collins, 1966.

The irony was that it was, to a great extent, Hauptmann's naivety and unsuspecting nature rather than his animal-like cunning (the Lindbergh version) that led to his downfall. In 1932 he went into partnership with another German immigrant, Isidor Fisch, who claimed to have a prosperous business selling furs and pies. In November 1933, having borrowed $2,000 from Hauptmann, Fisch returned to Germany, leaving a shoebox with his partner for safekeeping. A few months later, Hauptmann learned first that Fisch had died from tuberculosis and then that he had been a con-man whose 'businesses' were valueless shells. When he later opened the box, he discovered it was full of money and, thinking that he was entitled to keep it in view of all the money Fisch owed him, he kept it from his more scrupulous wife, hid it in his garage and started spending it at local shops. When the boss of his local gas station recognised the serial number on one of the notes as Lindbergh ransom money he contacted the police, who swooped on Hauptmann. The following day, the *Daily News* headlined 'Lindbergh Kidnaper [*sic*] Jailed', an indication of the widespread assumption that at last, after a two-year hunt, the guilty man, Hauptmann, had been apprehended. The police themselves certainly thought as much and set out to mount a case against Hauptmann while ignoring the only concrete lead they ever had – to Fisch. How had Fisch acquired the ransom money? Was he one of the kidnappers? Or had he merely bought the 'hot money' at a discount? These questions were never pursued. Nor did the police stop to wonder if a man who knew he had Lindbergh ransom money would spend it so openly at his local gas station, even telling the attendant that he had a hundred or so similar notes at home.

Not only did the police fail to pursue these lines of thought, they actively suppressed any evidence that led away from Hauptmann. But, apart from his connection with the ransom money, there was absolutely nothing to link him to the kidnapping and murder of Charlie Lindbergh sixty miles from his New York home. On a much grander scale, it was the same difficulty that confronted the Glasgow police when they arrested and charged Paddy Meehan for the murder of Mrs Rachel Ross. He and his colleague James Griffiths may have been called Pat and Jim, but there were no fingerprints, no bloodstained clothes, no witnesses.The police were convinced that they had their man, so they set about creating evidence with the help of a rigged identity parade and scraps of paper planted in Griffiths's coat after his death.

The American police under Colonel H. Norman Schwarz-kopf (father of General 'Stormin' Norman Schwarzkopf, who commanded the US Army in the first Gulf War in 1992) carried out exhaustive interviews with the Lindberghs' neighbours. Had they seen anyone acting suspiciously prior to the kidnapping? They drew a blank. Typical was one Millard Whited (as in sepulchre), who could be seen on Ludo's film, a cadaverous-faced shifty-looking character who might have been mistaken for a no-good villain in a Hollywood Western. Questioned by police the day after the kidnapping, Whited denied having seen anyone in the woods. But by the time of the trial, two years later, he identified Hauptmann as a man he had seen coming out of the bushes near the Lindbergh estate on two occasions in the days prior to the abduction.

It must have reminded Ludo of Mrs Crawley, the witness in the Luton case who initially told the police she had seen one of the gang from over her garden fence but would not be able to recognise him again, but who later in court gave a precise description of three men – height, hair colour and so on – and subsequently received £200 reward money from Commander Ken Drury. Likewise, Whited was reported to have been promised $150 together with daily expenses and a share of the reward money in exchange for his lying testimony. Another eyewitness who claimed to have seen Hauptmann, eighty-seven-year-old Amandus Hochmuth, was subsequently shown to have been nearly blind, later confusing a vase of flowers with a lady's hat.

But these villains were small fry compared with the prosecution's star witness, Charles Lindbergh himself, who sat in court throughout the trial thereby impressing on the jury his support for the prosecution team, members of which he lunched with regularly throughout the hearing. Lindbergh, readers will recall, had assumed control of the negotiations with the kidnappers and had accompanied the 'kindly old professor' Dr Condon to deliver the ransom money outside St Raymond's Cemetery in New York. Condon handed over the money while Lindbergh sat waiting in his car, about eighty yards away. He saw nothing, only hearing an unseen man shout, 'Hey, Doc!' in the darkness, to alert Condon to his presence. Two and a half years later, after listening to Hauptmann repeat those words while sitting incognito in a police station, Lindbergh swore that Hauptmann was the man he had heard that night. However, at the preliminary hearing at the Bronx County Courthouse, he admitted it would be very difficult to identify a man simply by hearing him say such a short phrase. Significantly, he later changed 'Hey, Doc!' to the more Germanic sounding 'Hey, Doctor!'

As Ludo wrote in *The Airman and the Carpenter*:

We can only speculate on the reasons that persuaded Lindbergh to change his testimony . . . [W]hatever the reasons, he took the stand and gave evidence that the voice he heard in St Raymond's was that of Richard Hauptmann. *From that moment Hauptmann was doomed.*[104]

It was a shameful thing to do . . . For, as Lindbergh himself had suggested in the Bronx, how could he say with any conviction that a voice he might hear now was

---

[104] Ludo's emphasis.

the same as the one he had heard in the dark at eighty yards' distance two and a half years before? What was it he had written at the time of his trans-Atlantic flight in defence of the dismissive way in which he was treated by the popular press? 'Accuracy means something to me. It's vital to my sense of values. I've learned not to trust people who are inaccurate. Every aviator knows that if mechanics are inaccurate aircraft crash. If pilots are inaccurate, they get lost – sometimes killed – in my profession life itself depends on accuracy.'

Was accuracy less vital because the life at stake now was not his own but that of the man in the dock? Was his sense of values to be discarded when applied to someone else? For millions of lesser mortals Lindbergh stood as the epitome of manly virtues, courage certainly but also truth, and when the world came to hear his evidence about the voice, they believed it to be the truth. Yet it was an untruth – not a deliberate lie like those that Schwarzkopf told, but an untruth. The man who was supposed to be – and in some ways had set himself – above the common herd had shown himself no better than the common herd. He of all people might have been expected to stand apart from the current stampede. Instead he had made himself part of it.

Careful readers of Ludo's book may notice that the word 'experts' above photographs of a group of crucial witnesses is printed in inverted commas. It was the kind of joke which would not have gone down well with American readers, who feel uncomfortable with flippancy in any form, but particularly in a judicial context. But Ludo had some experience with 'expert' witnesses, particularly since following and writing about the shameful cases of the Guildford Four and the Birmingham Six – two groups of men who were wrongly imprisoned for IRA bombings. In the case of the Birmingham Six – four of whom, like all of the Guildford Four, were represented by Gareth Peirce – the defendants were convicted partly on the evidence of forensic scientist Dr Frank Skuse ('a portly character'[105], according to Ludo), who claimed to have discovered nitro-glycerine on some of the accused men's hands, which was later proved to have come from playing cards. In the Lindbergh case the 'experts' included handwriting experts in the shape of the father-and-son team of Osborn and Osborn (the same firm that thirty years or so later confirmed Clifford Irving's hoax autobiography of Howard Hughes to be authentic). Like almost all the witnesses the Osborns backtracked from their original opinion that Hauptmann was innocent, apparently unaware that his misspelling of certain words matching the ransom notes had been dictated to him by the police. A more influential witness was the wood expert Arthur Koehler, who had volunteered his services to Lindbergh to examine the

---

[105] *Thirty-six Murders and Two Immoral Earnings.*

makeshift ladder used by the kidnapper(s) which had been left under the baby's window. The three interlocking sections consisted of several different types of wood, all amateurishly nailed together. 'It clearly was a job no man had taken pride in,' Koehler said. Still, after an exhaustive investigation which included writing to sixteen hundred pine mills on the East Coast, Koehler stated categorically that one rail ('Rail 16', as it was labelled) had been fashioned out of one of the floorboards from Hauptmann's attic. The ladder was produced in court and David Wilentz asked Hauptmann if he had made it. Hauptmann replied – and this can be seen on film – 'I am a carpenter,' which evoked one of the few laughs in the trial and clearly annoyed the prosecutor. In four simple words, Hauptmann had demolished hours of 'expert' testimony based on months of patient investigation. But it was another example of how something that is obvious to the layman carries little or no weight in a legal context. The obvious question remained unasked: why would a good carpenter make a bad ladder? Perhaps because he didn't want it to be identified as his handiwork? But, then, if it was a bad ladder it might be likely to break under his weight (as indeed happened). Would a professional carpenter really risk that? Once again we are in an Alice in Wonderland world.

Equally obvious, but again unasked, was the question: why would a carpenter with a stack of wood in his garage climb up into his landlord's attic (which involved entering a tiny linen closet, taking down the linen and the shelves and climbing up on the cleats through a fifteen-inch-square trapdoor holding a bunch of tools) in order to get just one length of wood for a makeshift ladder?(Ludo had seen for himself the improbability when he climbed up into the attic while making his BBC film.)

When published in America in 1985, Ludo's book was well received. 'One puts down *The Airman and the Carpenter* troubled,' wrote the critic of the *New York Times Book Review*[106], 'and certain that what was billed as The Trial of the Century was an awful miscarriage of justice.' The conservative *National Review*, 1985, concurred: 'The jury convicted him, but was he guilty? The answer seems to be almost certainly not.' Other reviews were equally enthusiastic, though there was an undercurrent of disquiet about Ludo's occasionally knockabout style. While accepting his arguments, *Newsweek*'s critic Peter S. Prescott wrote[107]: 'might not the same humanity which attracted him to Hauptmann's plight prevent Kennedy from calling the intermediary in the ransom negotiations [Dr Condon] "an old creep" who "sold out to the devil"? He calls other state officials "supreme asses" and the authorities who attempted to link the ladder to Hauptmann "these two jokers".' Likewise, Jim Fisher drew

---

[106] Jim Fisher, *The Ghosts of Hopewell*.

[107] 1 July 1985.

scornful attention in his book[108] to Ludo's description of the handwriting and timber experts as 'looking like senior members of an old folks' bowling club'.

Ludo would not have been surprised by any of this. He had anticipated a degree of hostility when writing in his introduction: 'Anyone who is prepared to go out on a limb and stand history on its head is bound to be an object of some resentment, especially if he is a foreigner.' To offset any hostility, he went out of his way to stress his admiration for the land of the brave and home of the free: 'I have known and loved America for more than forty years, travelled the length and breadth of it, been there on numerous BBC assignments. I know of no other country which I look forward more to visiting, nor one which gives me a greater sense of freedom.'

In the same confident spirit, Ludo embarked on a promotional tour of the United States hopeful that the book, his longest and his best, would have the same kind of effect that *Ten Rillington Place* had had in Britain. He was to be disappointed. The red carpet remained rolled up and there were setbacks all along the line. He arrived for a prime-time radio interview only to find that the station had cancelled it. Similarly, Philadelphia TV dropped a discussion programme with Anna Hauptmann. Even well-informed people, such as

---

[108] Jim Fisher, *The Ghosts of Hopewell*, p. 120.

the veteran Washington columnist Joe Allsop, who he expected to side with him about Hauptmann, did the very opposite. 'He was guilty as hell,' Allsop shouted down the line when Ludo rang him to enlist his help. 'Everyone knows that. And if you'd been around at the time, as I was, you'd have known it too.'[109]

And the antipathy was to continue over the years that followed. In 1987 a new book, *The Lindbergh Case* by Jim Fisher, the former FBI agent turned Professor of Criminal Justice at Edinboro University Pennsylvania, reasserted Hauptmann's guilt and damned Ludo's book as the work of a TV journalist whose BBC programme was 'a shameless piece of propaganda'. In response, Ludo savaged Fisher, calling him 'an ass . . . who styled himself Associate Professor of Criminal Justice (about which he was quite ignorant)', while labelling his book 'a shoddy and disgraceful piece of work which omitted all the new information that had come to light'.[110] More than a decade later, Fisher retaliated in his second book on the Lindbergh affair, *The Ghosts of Hopewell*. Ludo reviewed it for the *New York Review of Books*, but his article was finally rejected after the journal had held on to it for several months.

The final straw for Ludo came in 1998, when the US author A. Scott Berg won a Pulitzer Prize for his

---

[109] *Thirty-six Murders and Two Immoral Earnings.*

[110] *Thirty-six Murders and Two Immoral Earnings.*

massive, 618-page biography of Lindbergh. 'You would have thought,' Ludo wrote with obvious but justifiable bitterness, 'that the author of so comprehensive a book would have taken time out to study the case in depth and at least put forward arguments for a belief in Hauptmann's innocence. But no . . . Berg was too lazy, too cowardly or too ignorant even to attempt it and his tired conclusions were that, although his trial may have been unfair, there was no doubt that Hauptmann was guilty.'[111]

Ludo never got over his disappointment: 'It was the only one of all the cases I have looked into in a lifetime of investigating miscarriages of justice where, in seeking restitution for the wronged, I had to admit total defeat.'[112] Given that each of his three previous books – and particularly *Wicked Beyond Belief* – had had such a dramatic effect, it was not surprising that Ludo, who had spent three or four years on this much lengthier project, should feel disappointment, and even a little untypical bitterness. But in hoping to vindicate the Hauptmanns he had underestimated the forces he was up against. In contrast to Rillington Place, this was not a case of exposing the mistakes and offences of a small group of policemen, judges and politicians. The whole of America – from the President downwards – had been involved in the Lindbergh affair, with almost

---

[111] *Thirty-six Murders and Two Immoral Earnings*.

[112] Ibid.

every member of the police, the FBI, the press, the legal establishment and the American public all clamouring for Hauptmann's blood and rejoicing in his execution. A single book, particularly one written by a foreigner, was not going to change things overnight. And in the same way that the public had shown more interest in Christie's gruesome murders than in the innocent Evans's execution, the Lindbergh case had lived on over the years not as a story of a gross miscarriage of justice but as the starting point for a variety of often bizarre and unlikely conspiracy theories, only some of which involved Hauptmann.[113]

'I had to admit total defeat,' Ludo had written, but 'total defeat' was putting it too strongly and ignored the fact that there were others besides Ludo involved in the campaign to vindicate Hauptmann, most notably his indomitable wife Anna, whose efforts and those of her lawyer Robert Bryan had led to the release of all the police files relating to the case. These, in turn, had led to Anthony Scaduto's *Scapegoat*, with its detailed analysis of the doctoring and falsification of the evidence. Meanwhile, over the years since the case, the reputation of Lindbergh, like that of so many national heroes, had

---

[113] As recently as 2013, in *Cemetery John: The Undiscovered Mastermind of the Lindbergh Kidnapping*, Robert Zorn named another German, Johannes Knoll, as the chief of a gang of four that included Hauptmann. Zorn alleged that Hauptmann was recruited for his 'carpentry skills' (clearly a blunder, in view of the poor-quality ladder which broke).

been severely dented, particularly by his active support for the Nazis in the thirties, his campaign to keep America out of the war and his insistence that the Jews were behind the calls for US involvement – 'We cannot blame them for looking out for what they believe to be their own interests,' he told an anti-war rally, 'but we must look out for ours.'

Lindbergh was partially rehabilitated after the war, when he was finally allowed to rejoin the Army Air Corps, all of his previous requests having been refused. He wrote a best-selling account of his historic flight – *The Spirit of St Louis* – which was later made into a film starring James Stewart. But then, more than three decades after his death at the age of seventy-two in 1974, his reputation as the all-American hero – 'the idol of the twentieth century', as A. Scott Berg had described him – received a fatal blow when a book was published in Germany. Rudolf Schröck's *The Secret Life of Charles A. Lindbergh* (2005) revealed that Lindbergh had raised three clandestine families in Germany and Switzerland, fathering a total of seven children, five of them by two sisters, Brigitte and Mariette Hesshaimer, and two more by his one-time secretary, Valeska. None of the children had any idea who their father was until Brigitte died and a cache of 150 letters from Lindbergh was discovered. Why a man who was already the father of five children (in addition to Charlie) by his legitimate wife Anne should wish to raise yet more children with the help of three women remains a mystery. Equally puzzling was why Lindbergh, a keen eugenicist, should choose two sisters who had both been disabled by tuberculosis and were therefore unable to walk properly to bear his children.[114]

Whatever the truth, the story demolished the myth of a man whom Winston Churchill had once described as 'all that a man should do, and all that a man should be'. Instead, Schröck's book presented him as a weird and deeply unattractive character. Ironically, confirmation of this verdict can be found in Lindbergh's own, posthumously published *Autobiography of Values*, a book that is full of spurious profundity, along the lines of: 'Life and awareness fade when the death of an individual takes place – But does life itself – love, memory and reason – expand into the universe or withdraw into the atom with physical decay? Do qualities of spirit orbit on electrons? Are these qualities lured by molecular combinations from the emptiness of space?'

These two books led to much greater willingness among the American public to question Lindbergh's conduct in the kidnapping affair, in particular his role in bolstering the prosecution by identifying Hauptmann by his voice. At the trial, the airman's 'national hero' status had exercised a baneful influence on the police, the lawyers

---

[114] Charles Lindbergh, *Autobiography of Values*. (Harcourt Brace, 1978). 'A girl should come from a healthy family,' he wrote. 'My experience of breeding animals on our farm had taught me the importance of good heredity.'

and the jury, most of whom idolised him.[115] But once an element of doubt started to creep in, it was far easier to view Hauptmann as a falsely convicted scapegoat.

Looked at now, thirty years after it was published, *The Airman and the Carpenter* can be seen as ahead of its time. While not achieving the dramatic change of heart Ludo had been hoping for, his book, coming after a mass of books, most of them, even Scaduto's, peddling bizarre conspiracy theories of one variety or another, told the story for the first time in a way that made sense of it. As with *Ten Rillington Place*, it was not so much Ludo's detailed examination of the evidence – though there was plenty of that – which convinced the reader, but rather the pictures he painted of all the main characters, and especially the Hauptmanns, Ludo never having once wavered from his original conviction in his New York hotel bedroom.

It was the dramatic cohesion of *The Airman and the Carpenter* that appealed to the film producer Barbara Broccoli, who bought the film rights and commissioned William Nicholson who had previously scripted *Shadowlands* (on the life of C. S. Lewis) to write the screenplay. The resulting film, titled *Crime of the Century* and starring Ingrid Bergman's daughter Isabella Rossellini

---

[115] Shortly after the trial, juryman Howard Biggs admitted, 'When people like the Lindberghs and the Morrows say something you've just got to believe them' ('Why the Jury Voted to Put Him in the Chair', *Detroit News*, 15 February 1935).

as Anna Hauptmann, premiered in 1996. It is not often that an author praises the film adaptation of his book, but Ludo, who attended the premiere with Moira in New York, was an exception, expressing his full approval.

Yet six years later he was still irked that it had been left to a TV company to produce the film after all of the big Hollywood studios had turned it down: 'the puritanical element in the American psyche thinking it not right (and not box office) to question a verdict handed down in an American court by an American jury, exposing yet another American cock-up'.[116] Where now was his undying love of America and Americans that he had written about so movingly in the foreword to *The Airman and the Carpenter*?

> The reluctance of Americans ever to admit error, whether in correcting miscarriages of justice or in the fondness of their armed forces for opening fire on friendly troops or in the frequent cock-ups in everyday business or social life would seem to stem from the macho image they have of themselves and their philosophy of 'never apologise, never explain'. When a mistake is pointed out ... the inevitable rejoinder is the dismissive 'too bad!'.[117]

As Ludo's BBC documentary had revealed, Richard Hauptmann was allowed to make a statement to

---

[116] *Thirty-six Murders and Two Immoral Earnings.*
[117] Ibid.

camera after his conviction. Standing behind prison bars, he declared: 'I swear to God I am absolute [*sic*] innocent. I have told all I know about the crime.' The American public may have been surprised to hear this man – described only two days previously by David Wilentz as 'the filthiest and vilest snake that ever crept through the grass' – making a solemn oath to God. But this was not just a form of words for him. Nearly all of Hauptmann's final statements bear witness to a strong religious faith, matched only by that of his wife.

After the last-ditch efforts by Harold Hoffman, Governor of New Jersey, to secure a reprieve had failed and only hours away from his execution, he received a letter from Hauptmann, written in German:

> My writing is not for fear of losing my life, this is in the hands of God. It is his will. I will go gladly. It means the end of my tremendous suffering. Only in thinking of my dear wife and little boy, that is breaking my heart. I know until this terrible crime is solved, they will have to suffer under the weight of my unfair conviction.

Hauptmann then addressed the prosecuting counsel:

> Mr Wilentz, with my dying breath, I swear to God that you convicted an innocent man. One day you will stand before the same judge to whom I go in a few hours. You

know you have done wrong on me, you will not only take my life but also the happiness of my family. God will be judge between me and you.[118]

It is unlikely that this chilling message from death row caused David Wilentz any sleepless nights, any more than Ian Waddell's murder of Josephine Chipperfield would have worried Lord Robertson, who had set him free to murder again. Like many others involved in the Lindbergh case, Wilentz had been certain that Hauptmann was bound to confess before the end. He even gave his assent to the suggestion of Harold Hoffman, who had taken up Hauptmann's cause, that they would both agree to commute his sentence to life imprisonment if he confessed to his role in the kidnapping. With her passionate concern for truth and strong religious faith, Anna Hauptmann was shocked by the suggestion that her husband could save his life by telling a lie while Hauptmann himself realised that acceptance of the offer would mean life imprisonment as a self-confessed child-murderer and disgrace for his wife and son, whose only hope for the future lay in continuing to insist on his innocence and fighting for his pardon. There was no way out. He wrote one final statement in German:

---

[118] Anthony Scaduto, *Scapegoat*, pp. 421–2.

I am glad that my life in a world which has not understood me has ended. Soon I will be at home with my Lord. And as I love my Lord, so am I dying an innocent man . . . I am at peace with God, I repeat, I protest my innocence of the crime for which I was convicted. However I die with no malice or hatred in my heart. The love of Christ has filled my soul and I am happy in him.[119]

This was the man who Professor Jim Fisher later called a man of 'no conscience, no insight, no imagination, no perception and no feelings except greed and anger',[120] the man compared by Lindbergh to a wild boar and by Wilentz to the vilest snake. How was it possible that such a man facing imminent death could write so calmly of his love for Christ and his longing to be with his Lord? It seems that not one of Hauptmann's accusers has tried to answer the question, even if they considered it.

It is a sad fact that writers who have no religious belief or feel embarrassed by discussions of faith can brush aside or deliberately ignore religion's powerful influence in the lives of others. Ludo himself was not only a non-believer but a crusading atheist in his later years. So it is hardly surprising that there is almost no religious element in his account of the Hauptmanns, an omission that significantly weakens his argument. This

---

[119] *The Airman and the Carpenter*, p. 400.

[120] J. Fisher, *The Lindbergh Case*, 1987.

is particularly noticeable in an article he wrote for the *Independent* about Anna Hauptmann.[121] He praises her integrity, her strength of character, her lack of bitterness, the courage with which she faced life after losing her husband. But there is not a word about the faith that sustained her throughout. Yet Ludo had spoken to her, and he must have read the long interview with Anthony Scaduto that appears in *Scapegoat*:

> I believe in a God in heaven. I find out so many times. I get strength from that belief. If I didn't have this, I have nothing. It helped me survive. I don't complain. God has been with me all the time, all these years, that's all I need. To the last breath I have I know Richard was innocent and I'm not afraid to die, I'm not afraid of anything.[122]

Such passionately held faith put Ludo in the difficult position of admiring a woman whose most deeply held beliefs he regarded as nonsense. Where would that take him if he followed it to its logical conclusion? All his adult life he had been driven by a need to disprove the religion in which he had been brought up by his parents and later at Eton. This turned into an obsession as he grew older, and in 1999 he published *All in the*

---

[121] 3 December 1988.

[122] Anthony Scaduto, S*capegoat*, p. 474. She died in 1994 at the age of ninety-five.

Mind: A Farewell to God, in which he ridiculed all religions, but particularly Christianity. He dismissed the Gospel writers as 'great tellers of tales' and likened Jesus walking on the water to 'a music-hall joke'. To any reader who had admired his skill in examining and appraising evidence, his instinct for uncovering the basic truth of any story, this book was a sorry contrast. Unsure of his facts and citing obscure and eccentric witnesses to support his arguments, he flailed about, giving the impression of a man not expressing any heartfelt conviction but more of one desperately trying to dispel his own doubts or, in the case of Anna Hauptmann, unwilling to acknowledge the power of faith – even though to have done so would have greatly strengthened his case.

Chapter 5

On with my Coat and Out into the Night

Whether it was advancing age or disappointment over the American reaction to *The Airman and the Carpenter*, it proved to be Ludo's last attempt to right an injustice in book form. But he was still in receipt of countless appeals for help from prisoners, some of which he was unable to resist, if only to write about them in the press.

While continuing to help Gareth Peirce on behalf of David Cooper and Michael McMahon, Ludo also joined forces with her to fight for George Long, who wrote to him in 1987 after hearing him attack Britain's adversarial system of criminal justice during a radio interview. As in the Timothy Evans case, overzealous police officers had forced a confession out of Long and then presented it to the court during his trial for murder. Thanks to Gareth and Ludo's efforts, and those of his probation officer Christine Palmer, Long was eventually released in 1995, sixteen years after starting his sentence.

Ludo included an account of the Long case in *Thirty-Six Murders and Two Immoral Earnings*, a collection of pieces summing up all the cases with which he had been involved. He dedicated the book to Gareth Peirce, 'doyenne of British criminal defence lawyers whose sustained and untiring work behind the scenes on behalf of the innocent and wrongly convicted – among them the Birmingham Six, the Guildford Four, Cooper and McMahon and George Long – has led to large numbers of them seeing their convictions quashed and liberty restored'.

Looking back over the previous forty years, Ludo was able to note several reforms that owed a great deal to his campaigns. Most notable was the Police and Criminal Evidence Act of 1984, which put the police under a statutory obligation to tape-record the questioning of every suspect in a police station. Later, the Runciman Commission – set up by Tory Home Secretary Kenneth Baker in 1991 – resulted in the creation of the Criminal Cases Review Commission, an organisation that is independent of the police and has the power to refer cases to the Court of Appeal (as happened in the Cooper and McMahon case, leading eventually to their posthumous pardons). But the adversary system remained unchanged – two lawyers fighting a point-scoring duel rather than a single inquisitor, as in France, seeking to establish the facts – and, in spite of these reforms, there seems to be no end to miscarriages of justice involving police malpractice. For example in the Josie Russell case Michael Stone was convicted mainly thanks to the evidence of fellow prisoners who claimed to overhear him confessing – the same kind of bogus evidence used by Drury to convict McMahon in the Luton case.

Such has been the volume of alleged miscarriages of justice that the CCRC has recently decided to limit the number of cases it will investigate at any one time. Not surprisingly, this has dismayed campaigners, as has the Commission's decision to appoint retired police officers to examine evidence.

This one-step-forward-two-steps-back routine suggests an overall reluctance on the part of the public and the press to accept that the 'forces of law and order' are fallible and possibly even corrupt. In spite of all that happened in Ludo's lifetime and has continued to happen since his death, 'the integrity of the police' is still discussed in reverential tones, as something to be valued and preserved. It suggests that we all of us like to live with the comforting illusion that our police force and our legal system are an example to the rest of the world. So, when Gareth Peirce writes, 'It is not difficult to secure the conviction of the innocent,'[123] it is easy to understand why many people find the notion alarming, if not terrifying.

---

[123] 'The Framing of al-Megrahi' in *Dispatches from the Dark Side*.

Everything suggests that there are forces at work here which cannot be dealt with by Royal Commissions or bodies like the CCRC. With the Lindbergh case many may reassure themselves with the thought that Hauptmann's conviction and execution could only have happened in the unsettled, almost hysterical atmosphere of 1930s America. Yet the need for a scapegoat remains a powerful human instinct in the wake of any terrible crime. Witness what happened after the Lockerbie bombing in 1988, which resulted in the deaths of 270 people on board Pan Am Flight 103. An innocent Libyan, Abdelbaset Ali al-Megrahi, was found guilty in 2001 by a tribunal of three Scottish judges on the basis of evidence very similar to that which helped convict Hauptmann – a Maltese shopkeeper bribed by the Americans to identify Megrahi, suspect British 'experts' wrongly identifying fragments of an explosive device found at the scene of the crash, and the world's media happy to accept a ludicrous scenario in which terrorists would put a bomb in an unaccompanied case on a plane in Malta flying to Frankfurt, which was then transferred to a plane to Heathrow, where it was loaded onto Flight 103, finally exploding over Scotland. For years afterwards, Megrahi, regularly described as 'the Lockerbie Bomber', was vilified in the press, and there was an outcry when he was sent back to Libya, where he died from cancer. The small body of campaigners who had questioned the verdict – who were eventually vindicated twenty-five years after the bombing – included Paul Foot and Gareth Peirce, both of whom wrote powerful accounts of what Gareth called 'The Framing of al-Megrahi'. Yet, in spite of all the evidence provided by a defecting Iranian intelligence officer, many people, including the majority of the victims' relatives, persisted in believing in Megrahi's guilt.[124]

All of this came too late for Ludo, whose book *Thirty-six Murders and Two Immoral Earnings* was published in 2002, when he was eighty-three and struggling to cope with his wife Moira's decline. She had pursued a second career as a writer since giving up ballet and the stage. Her three published books included a biography of Ellen Terry, and she wrote countless book reviews for the *Daily Telegraph*. But in 1998 she had contracted viral encephalitis after suffering a mild stroke the previous year. It affected her speech, her understanding of events and her ability to help with the editing of Ludo's work, a task she had always enjoyed. In 2002, urged to do so by their four children, the couple moved from their house in Avebury, Wiltshire, to a residential home in Boar's Hill, Oxford, near to where their daughter Rachel was then living. Moira died shortly after her eightieth birthday, in January 2006. Ludo's own health had begun to decline by then, and in 2008 he moved to

---

[124] Ultimately, some were prepared to admit that 'he did not act alone'. A similar concession was often made by those who refused to accept that Richard Hauptmann was wholly innocent.

another residential home in Dorset, where Rachel was now living. He died in Salisbury on 18 October 2009 after an operation on a fractured hip following a fall.

It was consistent with Ludo's rather ambivalent attitude towards religion that his memorial service – on 1 December – was held in Christ Church Cathedral, Oxford. I was surprised and honoured to be asked to speak at the service, which, though conducted by clerics, had little or no religious content. Some years previously, I had written an obituary of Ludo for the *Daily Mail*, so I was familiar with the outline of his life story. He had also been quite closely involved with my magazine, *The Oldie*, during the 1990s. He had stood in for me at one point as *The Oldie*'s television critic and later created a minor sensation when he complained in a book review about the disproportionate number of black and Asian extras in BBC soap operas. He also starred in our short-lived *Oldie TV* series on BBC Two, in which he played the role of a grumpy old panellist complaining about such irritations as the awkward mannerisms of female weather forecasters.

During one of our programmes he had spoken of his desire to be buried at sea and he later repeated this in an *Oldie* feature titled the 'Death File', in which famous people were asked about their last wishes. I remembered this article when thinking about what to say at his memorial service. With typical self-deprecation, Ludo had rejected the idea of any elaborate obsequies. He certainly did not want anyone singing Frank Sinatra's 'My Way' – If 'I did it my way? What a stupid remark. You couldn't do it any other way.' As for a memorial service: 'That's really up to the living. Besides, a memorial service would depend very much on popular demand.'

And when it came to thoughts of life and death:

I don't know why we are here or where we are going, or what the point is – except what you make of life yourself. I've had a wonderful life and I wouldn't have missed it for anything. As far as death is concerned Hilaire Belloc summed it up best when he said in one of his poems – 'On with my coat and out into the night.'[125]

---

[125] *The Oldie*, 30 October 1992.

Books cited in the text

By Ludovic Kennedy

One Man's Meat (1953)

Murder Story (play) (1956)

Ten Rillington Place (1961)

The Trial of Stephen Ward (1964)

A Presumption of Innocence: The Amazing Case of Patrick Meehan (1976; 2nd edition 1977)

Wicked Beyond Belief (1980)

The Airman and the Carpenter (1985)

On My Way to the Club: An Autobiography (1989)

Truth to Tell: The Collected Writings of Ludovic Kennedy (1991)

All in the Mind: A Farewell to God (1999)

Thirty-six Murders and Two Immoral Earnings (2002)

By other authors

Gregory Ahlgren and Stephen Monier, *Crime of the Century: The Lindbergh Kidnapping Hoax* (1993)

Noel Behn, *Lindbergh: The Crime* (1994)

Joe Beltrami, *A Deadly Innocence* (1989)

Barry Cox, John Shirley and Martin Short, *The Fall of Scotland Yard* (1977)

John Eddowes, *The Two Killers of Rillington Place* (1994)

Michael Eddowes, *The Man on Your Conscience* (1955)

Nicholas Fairbairn, *A Life is too Short* (1987)

Jim Fisher, *The Lindbergh Case* (1987)

—, *The Ghosts of Hopewell* (1999)

Charles Lindbergh, *Autobiography of Values* (1978)

Patrick Meehan, *Innocent Villain* (1978)

—, *Framed by MI5* (1989)

Jenna Miscavige Hill, *Beyond Belief: My Secret Life Inside Scientology* (2013)

Harold Nicolson Diaries and Letters, 1930–1939 (1966)

Gareth Peirce, *Dispatches from the Dark Side* (2010)

William Sargant, *Battle for the Mind* (1957)

Anthony Scaduto, *Scapegoat* (1977)

Rudolf Schröck, *The Secret Life of Charles A. Lindbergh* (2005)

M. J. Trow, with an introduction by Ludovic Kennedy, *'Let Him Have It, Chris': The Murder of Derek Bentley* (1992)

Bob Woffinden, *Miscarriages of Justice* (1987)

Theon Wright, *In Search of the Lindbergh Baby* (1981)

Robert Zorn, *Cemetery John: The Undiscovered Mastermind of the Lindbergh Kidnapping* (2013)

Index

Index

Index

Index